Mindfulness in Action:

A Hands-On Guide to Creating Peace Amidst the Chaos

Sharon Sayler

To Christine
Enjoy the
adventure
Sharon
Say

"It's not the experience, it's the meaning you give to what's happening to you right now that determines your destiny. Are you living a half-experience or a heart-experience?"

~Sharon Sayler~

Preface

We are all here for the same purpose: to serve.

It is in how we consciously choose to express our service that we find our purpose(s).

An active awareness mindset isn't about believing, it's about Being. It is the enjoyment of all that life has to offer. Be grateful for both sadness and joy, for without sadness one would not understand joy. Commit to putting your heart, head and soul into the moment and make the choice to live mindfully aware. Set mindful intentions for this moment, your day and your life. Through each passing moment of time, either consciously or unconsciously, we change. We get to choose with each moment to be a new, more powerful being, ready to do greater things in the world. Find your explorer. Enjoy this moment, as there will never be another moment like this.

- Live consciously.
- Live courageously.
- Live mindfully and actively aware.

Now is as good a time as any... to live life with your senses open and savor the moment.

Free Mindful Action Poster: Visit
www.MindfulnessInActionBook.com/

What is Mindfulness in Action?

Many people think that mindfulness is meditation. It can be, and it also involves active awareness throughout your day.

Active awareness is what I call the simple everyday practice it takes to stay cognizant, aware and conscious throughout the day AKA mindful.

It is so easy these days to go about your day distracted. It seems as if being unaware of your surroundings is the new norm. How often do we see people walking down the street with their head down and eyes ·glued to a phone? At coffee the other day with a friend, the first thing we both did was put our phones on the table, within quick reach as if the fate of the world depended on us being in constant contact. His phone chirped first. It was a text, not urgent, but he felt compelled to answer it. Mine bonged, and with the same compulsion, I stopped our conversation and quickly typed a reply that turned into 4 more back-and-forth texts.

We looked at each other and laughed. We'd come to catch up and had been there ten minutes without any meaningful connection. The phones were immediately tucked away. We savored our time together.

He shared that a similar event happened while taking his children on summer break. As a single dad, he enjoys the extended time he gets with them including his annual family gathering of "all the in-laws, outlaws and cousins."

One morning he arose early to "get some work done." Shortly after he got "really into finally getting something done," his young daughter burst into the room to show him all the various bugs and small fish she and her cousins had caught down at the pond. Without thinking, he briskly waved her off. It wasn't until his daughter shuffled out of the room, head dropped and dejected, that his sister came up, tapped him on the shoulder and said, "You should have seen her face...you stomped on her joy."

In that moment, he knew his best intentions to spend real time with his kids had been sabotaged by not staying true to his intention. He was brought back to active awareness quickly enough to save the relationship with his daughter from his mindless snafu, yet how many times do we go about our day without someone to tap us on the shoulder and say, "Hey, wake up...."?

Active awareness is a two-part process: setting your intention and following through on that intention.

My new mantra for each event of my day is: JUST BE THERE! It's amazing the magic that happens when you commit to Just Be There....

A true story~

Perhaps you were like me and have thought, "I'd love to meditate, it seems like such a good idea, but who has the time?" I tried for years – I couldn't sit still long enough, all sorts of projects, needs and my ever-growing to-do list would run through my mind. My beloved Aunt Myrtle used to say about my younger self, "That girl has ants in her pants!"

Then one day not long ago, something strange happened that only came about through active awareness ~ I knew this moment was about to be important.

In the middle of one of the most freakish rainstorms I've ever experienced, I became "trapped" in an unusual import store. True story, the heavens opened and it rained 2.31 inches in a very short period of time. Even by Pacific Northwest standards that's a freakish rainstorm!

As the only shopper wandering about the hand-crafted masks, bowls of semi-precious stones, brightly colored drapes, and loomed fabric laced with the pure scent of sandalwood, I heard, out of the blue, a thickly accented, "Do you meditate?" Stuttering to explain my "ants in her pants" dilemma, this kindly unassuming shop keeper pulls out a cushion, looks out the window at the gully-washer and says, "Sit, let me show you how to calm the mind in under four minutes... we have time and your gentle spirit is asking me for it."

"Okay...." My lingering over the two-syllables held more than a hint of skepticism. Nevertheless,

6

intrigued, I obliged. The cushion was surprisingly comfortable and while I wasn't able to take a "lotus" position, he assured me it wasn't necessary. Settling my tushie into the surprising supportive place, he said, "Pull your body up and straight. Start at your tail and slowly straighten up through to the top of your head, as if you are tightening a rope — your lifeline. Your core must be comfortably engaged, as that is the center of it all."

"Now, gently position your left hand just above your mid-lap, right about your belly-button.

"Place your right fingers just over the left fingertips to create a little bowl. Now gently touch the tips of your thumbs together to create a little lid over your bowl.

"Close your eyes if you like and breathe in and out. Letting your lungs clear and expand from the bottom to the top - the breath feels like a wave softly rolling in and out.

"Gently and slowly.

"Breathe in and out filling your lungs with life-giving renewal.

"As you breathe in and out you notice your favorite place to rest.

"Over there across the way you see a luscious pool of water glistening with your favorite colors like tiny sparkles beaming, calling you over. The air is delicious; you savor it as you go explore what's here for you.

7

"You reach down and notice it's the perfect temperature. Curious, you gently put your toe into the water. Ahhh, perfect, now slowly step into the water and begin to immerse yourself.

"Feel it flow over you and about you.

"Savor the moment. It's the perfect temperature and the perfect salinity as you begin to float comfortably surrounded and supported. You are gently floating on the water, now. Safe and secure, you relax into the moment. Cherish it.

"Breathe in and out. Noticing with each exhale you release any stress in your body as this perfect pool of water supports and surrounds you.

"Breathe in and out. Slowly extending the length of each pause between your effortless inhale and exhale. Allow yourself to be completely immersed.

"Feel the perfect water surround your body, now your head. Your hair begins to float as you effortlessly drift below to be completely bathed in the shimmering warmth.

"Pause your breath. Continue your pause. You gently float below the water, deeper and deeper, continue to gently hold the pause of your breath....

"When you are ready, lift yourself to the water's surface, floating comfortably, and slowly exhale. Breathe in and out. On the inhale, pause, pause, pause....

"Now, float below the surface, going deeper this time... appreciate how the water supports you. When you are ready, gently float to the surface again knowing that you can float above or below at any time with ease and comfort...."

"Inhale for 5, pause, pause, pause, exhale to 7... keeping that gentle rolling wave moving throughout your body."

We did this five more times, each time holding the breath longer than before.... with an inhale, pause, pause, pause, float gently beneath the surface, then float to the surface, breathe in, pause, pause, pause and breathe out.

The key is to breathe in and out fully and completely with a pause between the inhale and exhale and again at the exhale and inhale (holding your breath). Inhale to a five count and exhale to a seven count in a rolling up and down motion....

On the inhale, start the expansion rolling at your lower belly and feel the rolling wave as you continue to fill your body with life-giving, cleansing breath. As you slowly exhale, roll the muscles of the chest down to the lower belly where you started the upward roll on your inhale. Keep the slow rolling inhale / exhale pattern going and gently open your eyes.

In what felt like just seconds, I heard, "Welcome back," noticing a wry smile as I opened my eyes refreshed and mentioned to him, "For the first time I had no monkey mind."

He smiled and said, "Monkey mind is impossible when your survival-mind believes you are drowning—that is why we gently float above and below the surface. Water can be very comforting to the conscious mind, yet the survival mind will only focus on your breathing." He was right; drowning never entered my mind as the water felt soothing as I gently floated above and beneath the surface, even though I'm not a great swimmer.

I thanked him, noticed that the rain had stopped and prepared to leave when he shared a parting thought, "You are a gentle soul, if I may, if you practice speaking your truth all will be okay." How'd he know....?

Be open to the moment unfolding; you may just get the gift of a lifetime like I did with learning a 4-minute meditation.

Quick meditations that focus on breathing work to settle your mind. When your mind is settled you can focus on the moment because the focused breathing has activated what's called the "rest-and-digest" response — the opposite of fight-or-flight, which is activated by shallow and rapid breathing. Shallow, rapid (fight-or-flight) breathing is considered normal breathing by far too many of us.

Mindfulness in Action is More Than Meditation

Breathe... and reflect for a moment, what did you experience in the 4-minute meditation?

Many report that even just reading my experience of the meditation slowed their breathing and calmed them. It's amazing what we can command our minds and body to do. Now, it is not just meditation, although meditation is great for resetting yourself mentally, physically and spiritually; it's also about being conscious or aware of something, paying attention on purpose, and knowing what's around you and what you do each and every moment. Being aware each and every moment is being aware of NOW and NOW and NOW! What a tall order!

How do you maintain awareness when "now" is every moment and when autopilot is so easy? First off, you don't. It's not possible to be consciously aware of what's going on outside you and consciously aware of what's going on inside you at the same time. It can sometimes feel like it, as it happens very fast, yet there is a split second between the time of an event outside and an internal understanding.

However, this doesn't mean you just throw up your hands and quit. The key is keeping a conscious awareness, or as I like to call it, "active awareness." Active awareness involves the five senses and the mind. Zen Buddhists believe that

11

the mind is the sixth sense. I'm intrigued by that concept.

In an over-simplified explanation, you gather all together all of the information from your senses in your mind. As the other senses bring in information, that information is labeled and brought to our conscious awareness through the mind — the mind acts as the filter by which we are actively aware. Now, that's not exactly what Buddhism means by the mind being the sixth sense, but when I heard the concept I thought, yes, that ties together how you deal with your inner reactions to the outer world. Using your senses to make sense of what you experience is the practice of active awareness, AKA "mindfulness in action".

We maintain active awareness through mindful action; with "action" being the key word.

Let's take, for example, your sense of hearing: when you hear a sound, your ears, and in turn, listening is part of what you use for awareness.

It will help your moment-to-moment awareness to look at your senses in unison... did you know hearing has been called "touch from a distance?" That's an interesting way to look at it, in that it creates similar soothing or dissonance responses. A mother's up and down rhythm of words often soothe an infant the same way a mother's touch does. These connections exist within all parts of us.

Another example is your inner ear (the part we use for balance) connects to the sensory systems that move our eyes. When you move your head to the left your eyes automatically move to the right to counterbalance and the same when you move your head to the right the eyes compensate by moving left. Amazing!

Back to your awareness, what you see, hear, touch, smell, taste and then how you feel and think about those observations, feelings, thoughts, beliefs, and etcetera are how you define your world. The key to mindful action is to take in all of the sensory input and make sense of it without labeling or snap judging.

It is well known that the mind uses a process called "deletions, distortions, and generalizations" or what I like to call "mind inventions" to make all the external data fit into its — the mind's — reality. The mind abhors the new and works hard to make what's happening in the moment fit into patterns and contexts that it knows and understands how to respond to. There is no one reality though, true active awareness is in knowing the context and patterns that you are experiencing and everyone experiences reality differently.

It's not always easy to stay in active awareness, but if you practice the following phrase it will take you far; "What did I see, hear and feel that led me to believe...<insert your label or judgment>?" You can add smell and taste too, but the shorthand

13

question to ask is "What did I see, hear and feel that led me to believe...<insert your label or judgment>?" When my long-time mentor Michael Grinder shared the above question with me, the need to make snap-judgments melted away. My views on being mindfully aware with my actions and conscious awareness of others' reality changed instantly.

Try this experiment: Think back to something or someone that you had an odd reaction to. Maybe you placed a label on them... even something as simple as, "They sure are quirky...." Notice that phrasing, placing a label *on* someone or something... it's similar to the reaction we unconsciously have when we say, "Talk *to* them" instead of "Talk *with* them." Words have strong meanings, even when you are just talking to yourself.

As you hold that event in context in your mind ask yourself, "What did I see, hear and feel that led me to believe...<insert your label or judgment>?" What are the first things that came to mind? Write them down.

Awareness becomes a lot easier when you learn to let go of reactivity and your mind-inventions. Repeat after me once again... "What did I see, hear and feel that led me to believe...<insert your label or judgment>?"

Finally, you will find that the majority of the suggestions in *Mindfulness in Action* are short. They are meant to stimulate conversation and reflection, not to be dogma or a mandate. Just like those dozen words that changed my world instantly: "What did I see, hear and feel that led me to believe...<insert your label or judgment>?" I hope you find moments of change within too.

Enjoy *Mindfulness in Action* and be sure and visit http://www.MindfulnessInActionBook.com/ to download the Action and Strategy Sheets that will help you implement mindfulness in action. You will also find a complimentary mp3 and Action Sheet for the 4-Minute Meditation.

"Whatever you can do or dream you can, begin it. Boldness has genius, power and magic in it."

~Johann Wolfgang von Goethe~

Table of Contents

"Life is not a journey to the grave with the intention of arriving safely and in a pretty and well-preserved body, but rather to skid in broadside, thoroughly used up, totally worn out, and loudly proclaiming ----WOW---- WHAT A RIDE!"

~Author unknown~
— humor and wisdom greatly appreciated

Why Mindfulness in Action?

Before we begin…

Note to self: Life is as hard as I wish to make it.

Know that mindful action is not something anyone can give you – you can learn skills like those I share here, but the decision whether or not to take action is already within you. There is always more to learn… as you master one step, asking the question, "What's next?" "What's next?" is a choice and by choosing to continue learning through actions and focus on practicing awareness (and joy) in all aspects of life —even "in the rain"—you unlock all that you are passionate about and now, take control to create the life you desire.

Yet, mindful action is not just about mastering a set of skills. When you master something, it often becomes a predictable routine, which you automate … and you ultimately take it — the skills — for granted... unless you continue to play, learn, discover, and explore.

An all-too-common trap to being truly mindful and engaged is that your "mental autopilot" takes over huge parts of your awareness. I'm not here to give your "mental autopilot" a bad rap — you need it to survive — can you imagine having to remind yourself to breathe in, breathe out.... However, when your ability to nonjudgmentally observe is hindered through using autopilot for too many things for too long, mindful awareness is lost.

Living mindfully does not overlook the future, nor live in the past — it transforms within each moment your hopes, dreams, your desires, your skills, your soul — to create clarity and focus on the present and to accept that the past can't be changed and the future is still unknown. Your life is right now—make the most of what's in front of you.

- How is our life now?
- What would you change if change were simple, easy and painless?

Enjoy Mindfulness in Action and be sure and visit http://www.MindfulnessInActionBook.com to download the Action and Strategy Sheets that will help you implement mindfulness in action questions. Many times taking the action of writing it down makes it more real.

"There is only one success: To be able to live your life in your own way."

~Christopher Morley~

Mindfulness in Action Quest

To live with Mindfulness in Action is to:

- Live consciously and courageously

- Resonate with love and compassion

- Awaken the greatness within you and others

- Accept who you are — know that you are whole

- Make conscious choices for your life

- Acknowledge that conflict and contradiction exist

- Shift expectations into preferences

- Observe without judgment and be open to learn

- Know that you did the best you could, with the permission level you had at that moment

- Give grace to yourself and others

- Accept the fact that we each view life with a unique set of filters

- Acknowledge and entertain new ideas without having to accept them

- Know you can change only yourself

- Show appreciation and gratitude

- Know that forgiveness is one of the highest forms of love

- Have the courage to stay present in the moment

- Be comfortable in the knowledge that there is no one reality

- Take care of the one body you've been given

- Have fun, practice joy and see humor in it all (because ultimately, we aren't getting out of this alive).

Remember:

- Perfection does not exist — if it did, wouldn't it be boring?

- Setbacks will happen — more often than you will like

- Everything takes longer than you thought — and costs more than you want

- Everyone thinks they are doing what they should be doing. We all work from positive intention. Positive intention doesn't mean it's for the greater good though....

Share your ideas with me and download your copy of the Mindfulness in Action Manifesto at www.MindfulnessInActionBook.com/.

"Life will pass you by if you let it."

~Don Pickens~

All We Have Is This Moment

My friend Don Pickens loves to remind me, "Life will pass you by if you let it."

The "great gurus" tell us to stay in the moment... and I encourage you to take their advice. I know it's not as easy as it sounds though. It does get easier and easier with practice, so play with ways to make it easy.

I've found a little mantra that works for me to stay in the moment. My "mantra" is a paraphrase of the ending of the movie *Way Of The Peaceful Warrior*, scripted from the wonderful book by the same name written by Daniel Millman. My mantra is: "Here. Now. The Moment..."

"Here, Now, The Moment" reminds me to focus on the now, within that moment, rather than future pacing or past ruminating. Mantras can snap you back to the moment as all too often autopilot kicks in and moments creep up on us and surprise us.

Surprise is the enemy of being present! Surprise takes you out of the moment and catapults you into the past and/or the future with thoughts like, "What just happened?" "What does that mean?" and "What will happen next?"

Wouldn't it be great if we had a soundtrack behind each moment of our life (just like the movies) to warn us of impending doom?

A soundtrack to motivate you when needed, those creepy violins to warn you when something bad is about to happen, or the whispery sounds of harps to gently mellow you into meditation....

- What would your "in the moment" soundtrack be?

- What mantra will you use to snap you back into the now when you wander from the current moment?

Enjoy Mindfulness in Action and be sure and visit
http://www.MindfulnessInActionBook.com / to
download the Action and Strategy Sheets that will
help you implement mindfulness in action
questions. Many times taking the action of writing
it down makes it more real.

"The simple, but not so easy cure for living on autopilot is to consciously breathe!"

~ Sharon Sayler~

Back To This Moment

Know that how we choose to live in mindful action is as individualized as each one of us. Yet, living mindfully contains one common element – being committed to really live each and every moment your life gives you… but it's not always that easy.

The challenge is to fully live each moment — to stay present no matter the chaos, and to find passion, purpose and joy in each experience. But how?

Donna was just about to be introduced to give a speech in front of a thousand people — her largest audience to date — when she received a text message saying there was an emergency at the office. Certainly not the best time nor the best place to get such a text. Immediately, she was propelled out of that moment.

Immediately she was propelled out of her speech, her introduction — that moment she had expected would e the next moment — then SURPRISE!

When something happens to take you out of the moment, or you feel less than 100% confident and in control, use one or more of the following behaviors to snap you back into the moment, reclaim your power and reinforce your own confidence.

Your thoughts, emotions and actions/behaviors are a feedback loop. For Donna, she shared with me that even though moments earlier she had felt prepared, that single text message sent her both physically and mentally swirling about with a bad case of "jitters, butterflies and nerves."

When that happens, which it often does, the trick is to get your butterflies flying in formation!

You counteract those "jitters" with one or more of these five quick and specific techniques to bring you back to the moment and transform your thoughts, emotions and behaviors so that you once again choose the way you want to react.

These five actions will all bring your body back to the present moment so that you can consciously have your body send messages of calm to your mind. Quickly, the mind begins to shift to calm.... Amazing, how it works! Just doing one of these will pop you right back into the present moment (conscious) "driver's seat."

Present Moment Power Move #1: The Wet-Dog Shake, just like a golden retriever after a great splash, have a good shake! From top to bottom, shake the whole body, shake out your arms, your hands, your legs and feet...this is my favorite for a quick recovery back into the moment.

If the great shake is too much or would be too obvious for the situation, bounce a few times on the balls of your feet. You can add s backward shoulder roll too for extra zip. A backward shoulder roll is when you lift your shoulders towards your ears, press the shoulders back, and then drop them quickly to create a rolling movement. The shake, the bouncing feet and the backward shoulder roll work well to reset your awareness.

Present Moment Power Move #2: Cold water splashed on your face, swished around your mouth and/or an ice-cold water bottle pressed against the inside of your wrists will also bring your back to the present. It's not always easy to splash cold water on your face however swishing cold water around your mouth is socially acceptable and easy to do. And in a pinch, just pressing something ice-cold to the inside of your wrists will bring you back quickly too.

Present Moment Power Move #3: Spread out. Research shows the way you show confidence, leadership and dominance is to take up a lot of space — it also takes a conscious effort to make yourself "bigger.". They are called "power poses" in body language. A power pose is best defined as "any movement that is assuming an expansive posture."

Expansive poses elevate your testosterone (what they call the dominance hormone) and decreases your cortisol (one of your stress hormones) leading to increased feelings of confidence, control and power. It can take as little as one-to-two minutes to effect these hormonal changes. A quick turn-around for sure....

35

Present Moment Power Move #4: Laughter really is the best medicine. "Giggle," yes, giggle, even a forced giggle will bring you back to the present moment. If you can manage a real good laugh at what just happened you will find a side benefit of a vigorous workout to your chest, back and abs and strengthen your heart. It's been suggested that regular laughing boosts your immune system too.

Giggling or laughing will also reset your breathing pattern, relax your face and chest muscles and give you an overall feeling of happiness even a joyful "buzz" to bring you right back to the moment.

Present Moment Power Move #5: Breathe in through the nose and blow (exhale) out through the mouth. Inhale through your nose, slowly and fully and exhale with an extended exhale through your mouth. Your exhale is when you relax, and when you relax, you are able to some back to the present moment and those around you will relax as well. The most useful nonverbal I've learned is how to control my breathing. Reminding myself to breathe naturally and comfortably, no matter the situation, delivers a nonverbal message of confidence and poise. Breathing is the most often overlooked and underestimated nonverbal.

Breathing is more than supplying oxygen to your lungs. It profoundly influences your mood, how your brain functions, how sensitive your nerves are, and how tired or alert you feel even your "fight or flight" response. How you are breathing is contagious too. It directly influences those around you.

Given the unknowns and sometimes craziness that happens all around us, the key to staying present at all times is to breathe, yes *breathe* through each moment. Complete, deep, 360-degree breathing, where you feel your ribs and even your back expand.... This kind of breathing keeps you present through an experience. When we experience a surprise, a shock, or an unknown, all too often, we find we are holding our breath and activating our fight-or-flight response!

Do a little experiment. Quickly sniff (short rapid inhales through the nose) 10 times. What are you feeling right now? Most people feel a twinge of anxiety. That is the beginning of the fight-or-flight response. Monitor your breathing from time to time to make sure your breathing is sending a message of confidence and comfort.

Here's another experiment. Observe the effects of your breathing on others. Silently observe their breathing and your breathing; change your breathing pattern and see if the other person begins to mimic your breathing pattern. This may take a minute or two but play with it. You will find it interesting how easily your breathing pattern can affect another person.

People under stress often start rapid breathing by holding their breath. Then, as they need to breathe, they constrict their chest muscles, which causes shallow breathing. When the lungs fill only partially, the body needs to get more oxygen. This increases the speed at which they breathe.

Those stuck in a rapid breathing pattern often sound afraid or angry, as the pitch and volume of the voice rise with the change of airflow. They are also at a loss for words and frequently use verbal pauses or fill-in sounds, such as "uhm" and "ahh."

Some of the telltale nonverbals of rapid breathing and the resulting lack of oxygen—besides turning blue and passing out (which, of course, is a medical emergency!)—are when:

- Movements appear jerky and stiff
- The voice sounds different, forced or shrill
- Shoulders move up and down at a rapid pace
- The head moves backward and forward at an exaggerated pace

Low, abdominal breathing is the natural pattern in normal situations. The purpose of consciously breathing with long, slow, deep abdominal breaths is to bring the carbon dioxide and oxygen levels back in balance. It does not take too many rapid breaths to get your body's carbon dioxide and oxygen levels out of balance.

Breathe! Just breathe....

Critical to know: 360-degree breathing amplifies your current experiences and it can seem to slow down time. Try this: Take a moment to bite into something savory, take a deep breath and feel the savor.

As you begin to consciously and fully breathe, you may begin to experience emotions you are unaware of or thought you had dealt with. Know that this is normal and just breathe through them. There is joy in the tears... savor the awakening, let the emotions, just like your breath, flow through you and from you as you are relearning how to breathe the way the universe intended — fully and completely.

- How do you feel now?

    Breathe....

"Courage is like a muscle. We strengthen it by use."
~Ruth Gordon~

Practice Courage

Did you know that COURAGE is a "muscle"? Well, technically not, but play along with the metaphor. It's like a muscle because the more you use it, the stronger you get!

"Courage" is a word that has always fascinated me. Even thinking the word I feel stronger.

It takes courage to continue to move forward in the face of hardship, discomfort, long-odds, failures and discouragement. Yet, we see courageous acts all around us everyday.

I've found numerous descriptions of where the word "courage" originated. Most agree that the Latin root of the word is "cor"— which translates to "for heart." Then the descriptions take many different paths. One of my favorites is: "Courage comes from a French translation meaning 'rage of the heart.' It originated with horses that had to jump over something. In order to do so successfully, they have to send their heart over the fence first and then the body follows," from my friend and executive coach, Ann Masur Singer. Another favorite: "Courage originally meant, 'To speak one's mind by telling all one's heart,' from Brené Brown, author of *The Gifts of Imperfection*. It's amazing what you learn about yourself when you courageously push your potential. Here are a few ways to practice courage:

41

Be imaginative. Choose outside your box. If you feel a little tweak or twinge, then you are thinking outside your box.

Be brave. Move outside your comfort zone – even if just a smidge…. Anaïs Nin was right when she wrote, "Life shrinks or expands in proportion to one's courage."

Be adventurous. Raise the bar on what you think you can do. Too often our thoughts of "Oh, I could never do that…" limit what we really can do.

Be impeccable. Commit to being faultless with your words and deeds. Keep your promises to yourself. Keep your commitments to others.

Be focused. Bright shiny objects are all around us. Cultivate an environment that allows you to stay focused on one thing at a time. Use your breath to have a relaxed presence and focus on each moment.

Be actively aware. Choose to stay in the moment. Know what you want and need. Pay close attention to your reality and the reality of others – they are not the same thing. Keep asking yourself, "What did I see, hear and feel that led me to believe…<insert your label or judgment>?"

Share your ideas with me and download your copy of Ways to Step Into Your Courage at www.MindfulnessInActionBook.com/.

How will you practice courage today?

"Amazing things happen when you let them."

~ Sharon Sayler~

Change Always Starts With a Choice

Mindful or not mindful, actively aware or blissfully unaware, change when you wish, if you wish... only you know when the time is right.

Change is a choice and it can come in many ways. Remember the Law of Cause and Effect formula and ask yourself:

+ What is the effect I want to have right now?

+ What is the cause(s) for or of the effect?

+ What will the likely outcome(s) be?

+ Is that what I really want?

Your Choice

Be open to learning... set mindful intentions, outcomes, dreams and desires for this moment, this day and each day of your life.

Be open to receiving what you ask for in multiple or unusual ways.

Share your ideas with me and download your strategy sheet of the Law of Cause and Effect Questions at
www.MindfulnessInActionBook.com/.

"Give thanks for what you are now, and keep fighting for what you want to be tomorrow."

~Fernanda Miramontes-Landeros~

The #1 Thing Your Soul Needs

Many people are at war with themselves. A bold statement I know— but I've been there. It was 1998, my life was falling apart before my eyes, or so I thought. It felt real and it was real.

My two-decade long marriage was falling apart and my Southern Baptist upbringing was at war with what I was feeling and what I knew I had to do to save my sanity. The shaming head-chorus wouldn't stop, even though I'd left the church ten years prior.

I was allowing "outside" voices to reside in my head and they began to consume me. I had the same reel on repeat, with phrases such as, "He's really a good man," "He didn't mean it…." "He's a good provider…" and "How can you do that to your family?" I heard these voices over and over, but in my heart I knew what I had to do to save my family and myself.

Late one night, driving home in a pounding rainstorm, the pivotal mind-battle began. I couldn't breathe, my heart was racing and then it happened, , I could barely see – the rain was coming down in sheets….

Knowing I had to survive for my two sons, I made my way to the side of the road (I have no idea how.) There on the side of that dark stretch of road I thought I was going to die, right then and there.

It felt like it went on forever. It was the longest and loneliest 30 minutes of my life.

When you think you are dying, you make many a life altering decision — the most profound that night was to let it go, to stop trying to control everything.

All I wanted was to feel safe... and it seemed like a strange decision, but I chose to let it all go. I couldn't control anything, let alone everything! In the instant of letting go, I gained clarity. That moment, when swirling all around me was myself gasping for breath, I heard a voice inside my head ask me two questions:

- What part of this is yours; what part of this can you really control?
  "Only me, only how I choose to react..." flashed through my head.

- If that is true, whose permission are you waiting for?

What do you need right now?

"All the soul wants is to feel safe and loved, too many people look everywhere but within for both."

~ Sharon Sayler~

Looking Outside Will Never Get You What You Want

"Looking for love in all the wrong places..." As is so eloquently stated in that country song by Johnny Lee.*

Your conscious mind doesn't like the unknown; it might not be safe, so your conscious mind works hard to reject any and all opportunities because it doesn't want you to step into the unknown. Heaven forbid, you change!

Surprisingly though, the mind is a sucker for quick fixes. It loves to avoid the temporary discomfort of dealing with your deepest thoughts, hurts and fears. Your subconscious loves the words "simple," "quick" and "easy" because it tricks you into thinking that you are doing something — when in reality you are sidetracked from what you say you really want. The real opportunities for growth are the ones you feel most resistant to.

Mistakenly, you are often taught through fairytales and other lore to believe that all your fears will disappear once you get that perfect "item" or when your white knight or princess appears, but what happens on the outside only intensifies those wounded places on the inside.

A friend never attended college right out of high school, much to the disappointment of his father. My friend, by then in his thirties, decided to go back to school. He could only do it part-time due to other life commitments, so it took several more years than the average four to complete. In those ensuing years, his father passed on. When graduation finally came, we were standing at his graduation party, and he turned to me and said, "I thought I'd feel different, I thought I'd feel changed...." The problem was that he didn't need the degree for his chosen profession; he wanted the degree to finally please his dad.

Personally, I used to suffer from what I call "same-man-different-body" syndrome. I'd explain ad-nauseam to my friends about how each guy I chose was different — how they, my friends, just didn't understand.... But oh, they did understand, more than I knew.

One day, while walking along the beautiful Lewis River with my mentor and dear friend Michael hearing my stories again, he stopped, and said, "You are right, they are all very different except for the one way that matters most."

"I think they all loved me the best they could!" I protested. He nodded and with a wry smile, twirled a small stone through his fingers. He turned to examine the rough waters in front of us and shared, "They all live in the safe place of being emotionally unavailable." With that, was a loud SPLASH as the stone hit the water. Those words and that splash resonated through my mind. I heard the words and consciously knew what "emotionally unavailable" meant, but had no idea what he meant or how I would know "emotionally unavailable" the next time I saw it.

I've since learned that it manifests in me as a feeling of not being able to get close to the one I love, a feeling that there is always something in the way. I've spent these ensuing years discovering what it really means to be emotionally available. What I've learned is that there is an amazing freedom in being emotionally available and finding those in your world who are also emotionally available. It is with those people that you feel safe sharing your life.

Imagine that!

- What (or who) have you placed in your life that supports your problems?

- What does everyone around you see that you refuse to see?

Note to Self: I'm the only common denominator in my repeat problems.... Guess that makes me the one that has to change!

Get your Action Sheets at
www.MindfulnessInActionBook.com/.

* "Looking for Love" was written by Wanda Mallette, Bob Morrison and Patti Ryan and recorded by country singer Johnny Lee in 1980 for the soundtrack to *Urban Cowboy*.

There will always be reasons to wait... The truth is, there are only two things in life, reasons and results, and reasons simply don't count."

~Robert Anthony~

You Have The Power To Be; Seize It.

Do you have clarity or chaos? Chaos is a loss of your power and is the result of jumping right into an emotional overreaction. Emotional over-reactivity goes by many labels all the way from "Drama Queen" to "Chicken Little". When we react without being aware of why we are reacting, it is easy to emotionally overreact, leading all too often to more chaos.

The most common ways to recognize emotional over-reaction and its chaos are the after effects of fear, frustration, worry, doubt, guilt and hurt feelings.

Emotional reactivity is part of who we are. It happens in an instant and isn't something you work to eradicate, you work to be mindful of it and its triggers. Accept it. Embrace it. Breathe through it. It's through the conscious awareness of your emotional reactions that you are able to be mindful in your actions.

Know you are not your reactions. You choose how quickly you move through your reactions and emotional chaos to clarity. Clarity appears when we have the information we require to be in alignment with who we are in this world and knowing what we value.

Nothing outside of us has true power over us until we let it. Practice sadness or practice joy. Practice discontent or practice presence. It's all a conscious choice. Mindfulness in Action is based on three premises:

Now is the only time. A mindful life is created one step at a time. Practice being present in all moments—even when thinking of the future and reviewing the past. Consciously choose when you look forward or back. "I'm the one that has the choice of what experience I have now." Stay here, now.

Walk with grace. There is more than one choice for your life. Give yourself the same love and care you would your best friend — what I call "grace," as you enjoy this time to freely explore your interests, dreams, desires, purposes, passions and especially give yourself grace as you uncover your "operating-system-bugs".

Fine-tune your focus. We create what we focus on, whether it is what we want or not. If you focus on what you don't want, don't be surprised to get more of it. Each choice allows you to refocus and correct your course, if desired.

Many of the problems I hear from my coaching clients are not the real problem. The real problem is that they are lacking clarity on "what just happened" and they jumped right to reactivity.

Stop, breathe and say whatever is true for you right now. Step into as many of the multiple viewpoints as possible and again ask from each viewpoint whatever is true for them right now. Ask for feedback to fine-tune your focus, and give others the benefit of the doubt — grace. Know that now is the only time you really know you have.

Stop settling for chaos. Life is too short for that. Seek clarity; it is with clarity that you seize your personal power. Make a more mindful choice now.

- In what places in your life are you currently needing clarity?

- Is what you settled for taking up space for what you really want?

Free Mindful Action Strategy: Visit
www.MindfulnessInActionBook.com
for your Power Strategy Sheet

"The purpose of passion is to find your purpose."
~ Sharon Sayler~

Your Gifts, Your Skills, Your Passion and Your Purpose are not the Same

Let me explain: Natural gifts are what make you, you and they are also called "traits".

Skills are what you've learned through your life; they may be enhancements to your gifts or not. Just because I know how to roof a house doesn't mean that it's a natural gift, a passion, or a purpose. It's a skill I've learned. Yes, I really do know how to roof a house...but that's for another story.

It's important not to mix up purpose and passion. A passion is a strong desire for something, while your purpose is what you choose to do with the sum of your passions, gifts and skills.

We all have natural gifts and learned skills that are expressed through our chosen purpose(s) or in other words, the way we choose to be of service in this world.

There is no one purpose. Purpose(s) are not mutually exclusive — we're not talking about an either/or proposition.

My purpose to my sons is not the same as my purpose to my friends, or to my business associates. Many popular writings suggest that you find your one purpose or passion and all will be right with the world. Sorry... but it is not so. I have had the same natural potential and traits my whole life, but they have manifested themselves in multiple passions with multiple purposes.

For example, if your passion is to "save the whales," what is your purpose within that passion? Are you a writer who can spread the word or a biologist who desires to do research?

Passion and purpose are not the same and are constantly changing throughout your life.

- What are your passions and purposes within those passions?

How are you finding your gifts, passions and purposes right now?

"Don't be scared to be different, being the same is way more terrifying."

~ Jeff Hardy~

Words Are Magic and Other Life Challenging Moments

Have you ever shared a passion, desire, goal or dream and heard someone say, "Get real! Be realistic…." or something similar? Learn from and find joy when you feel challenged within those moments. It's those kinds of moments that bring clarity.

When Sam, my college advisor, told me I was "too old" and that I'd "never make it in the graphics industry," I replied, at least in my mind, with, "How dare you… I'll show you."

It's the "How dare you" moments in my life that have been the start of some of my greatest successes and experiences…strange, but true. What about you?

This "I'll show you" reaction is called a polarity response. A polarity response is defined as "a response that reverses, negates, or takes the opposite position of a previous statement." In other words, when we are told to do something, we do just the opposite. I'm sure you can see that this response has both positive and negative consequences.

Have you ever started a new diet, and made a commitment that this time you were going to stick to it? You were eating more than enough calories to sustain you and yet you still felt hungry and deprived? It's because we all have a "little evil twin" sitting on our shoulder that takes over when it hears a restriction, boundary command, or pronouncement. That little twin then stomps its foot and says, "No, that's so not me!"

The "No, that's so not me!" can work in the positive as well. Back to the story of Sam and my "No, that's so not me!" response. Two years later, I was invited back to share with the senior graphics class "How To Make It As A Freelancer". You see, less than two years after graduation, he'd seen my name in the local Business Journal as the designer for a conference given by the Clinton White House. Sometimes, things just align in your favor. Woohoo to alignment!

If you are on the other side of the table and having to deal with a polarity responder, use a language pattern of putting everything you say in the negative and throw in the word "but..." to get a polarity responder to see your point of view. For example:

"You will probably not agree with me, but..."

"You are probably are not going to like this, but..."

"This probably won't work, but I wanted to see what you think."

- What are those moments that changed everything for you?

Make note here as you observe yourself over the next week and see where you use a polarity response.

"All of us were meant to be happy and successful. Life is more than a two-week vacation once a year. It is, and can be, exactly what you want it to be. There are no limits except those you put on yourself."

~Thomas D. Willhite~

Uncover Your Soul Explorer

Discovering your potential, your passions and your purposes is the process of life. Your passions and life's purposes will most likely change over time. As you survey the whole, know that you can always tinker with the parts... listen to the questions and answers of your heart.

Give yourself permission to experiment and experience. For example, every year for my birthday, I challenge myself to a new adventure, one that I normally would not consider. For my 50th birthday, I tried pole dancing and loved it. That's hard work spinning around and not flying off... what a workout! I still love to do it. Then, it was rock climbing. I had fun but I didn't love it. Learning to shoot sporting clay was challenging and strangely stress relieving PULL! I tried to ride a motorcycle and realized when my son graduated at the top of the class and I was the only one that had failed that maybe popping wheelies was not for me.... The motorcycle school seemed to take a dim view of someone who kept falling off and as they said "laying it down." I learned that road rash is not my thing, but that's okay, the point is really in the exploration and learning.

- What have you always wanted to try?
- What's stopping you?

Go for it. We all define adventure and explore the world differently. Susan was born in the city, but had loved the high desert country for years. About fifteen years ago, she packed up and moved there without knowing a soul. She has been there ever since and has made a very happy life for herself. Some might say that was a bit radical, pulling up stakes and changing her entire life, but it worked for her.

- What will work for you?

What are you longing to explore right now?

"If you don't like how things are, change them! You're not a tree."

~Jim Rohn~

Bumping Up Against "Things"

As you start to become aware of all that is happening in the now, you may bump into your secret and not-so-secret fears. Perfect! You must establish where you are before setting a course for where you want to BE. Notice I didn't say "go"... BE tells your unconscious mind that it is within your reach. You will be there, just not yet, while "go" implies you will not reach it, as you are always going there and never arriving.

Sometimes, the biggest obstacle is you and the long-held presuppositions and preconceived notions about what you can and can't do — too often those notions stop us. Uncovering the parts, voices, notions and beliefs can be tricky. The mind is good at hiding them from our conscious Self. The mind is very content in its comfort zone — that's why it's a "comfort" zone!

Most often, to get what you want, you have to leave that comfort zone, at least on occasion. As you begin to focus on those long-held presuppositions and preconceived notions, begin to notice if your beliefs, thoughts and life become lighter and easier.

Listen carefully and notice what you feel as you work through those presuppositions and preconceived notions. This is where you can often uncover your cultural conditioning(s).

You often learn your presuppositions and preconceived notions in childhood and carry them around your whole life as if they were true. I'm always amazed at the presuppositions and preconceived notions I continue to bump into — savor those awareness "Aha moments". They are often life changing.

Awareness is the first step in finding and changing limiting patterns of behavior too. As you go about your day, just notice how old beliefs that no longer serve you have worked their way into your "operating system" and have become less-than-useful or even bad habits.

• Is it time to update your awareness?

Where are you right now?

"Too many people overvalue what they are not,
and undervalue what they are."

~Malcolm Forbes~

Familiarity Rarely Breeds Contempt,
It Breeds Indifference

There is an old saying: "Familiarity breeds contempt." Yes, it's true, familiarity can breed contempt, yet I have found that contempt usually comes from unmet expectations that may or may not be preceded by indifference. The longer we are around someone or something, the more inclined we are to find fault with it, but contempt usually flows through a sea of indifference first. Indifference is the signal that we have just given up on "fixing those faults," then often disappointment sets in from the unmet expectations and the first signs of contempt set in — if we let it.

When indifference festers long enough, it can breed contempt. But indifference can be just as fatal as contempt and often leaves us wondering about our own sanity. Contempt is easy to see and feel, while indifference isn't always so easy to spot.

Every day, my friend Diane and I would have to stop at the donut shop as we walked to high-school and every day I would joke, "You should just get a job here, and then you could have all the donuts you want...." Well, she did get a job there and within two weeks she never wanted to eat another donut again! I guess it was too much of a good thing....

Whether it's your donut job, your career, your business or a relationship, indifference is a slow, lingering energy drain.

Think about the first time you met someone and fell fast in love. Remember how wonderful it was when you first met? Were you captured just by their smile, their laugh and their presence? It felt wonderful, didn't it?

The more you shared, the more wonderful it felt. Then slowly something changed. The change is subtle; it's not that you are upset, have hurt feelings, or are angry or frustrated.

It — the relationship and that once special person — just felt different. You still cared about them, but the thrill, the zip, that special spice was gone... what happened?

Sure, you knew long ago that they have "baggage" and faults. That's okay, nobody's perfect. In fact, they had idiosyncrasies that were downright irritating! That was okay. They were worth it. That's okay, you said, "Nobody's perfect, including myself...."

However, what you do notice is that it's different and for you, that's not okay. What is it?

It's the start of being so familiar with someone or something that they are no longer special. You take them for granted and that's the beginning of indifference. Now all those once special things are "just them." It's expected. For example, "That's just Joe," or "Sue is always sweet like that." No longer do you notice that they always "do that special thing" or that you are "feeling twitterpated" when they hug you. Why don't you continue to see it as special after a while? We rarely remember what we expect until we don't receive what we expected.

Because a new "high-bar" has been set and it's just who they are and what they do - it's expected! When it's familiar and expected, it's not that the familiarity bred contempt; it bred indifference, thoughtlessness and ungratefulness. It was no longer special or noteworthy.

If left untreated, it will breed contempt, whether it's a relationship, a donut or your career.... Those times when it becomes a bit too expected or predictable are necessary times to think out-of-the-box for a moment and change the routine in a way that will be truly enjoyed. Think back to your "why."

If it's a relationship that's a bit stale or indifferent, why did you choose that relationship at the beginning? Think back and start by saying "thank you" once again for the little things that do make the other person special and see what happens.

If it's your job, career or business, think back to your "why." Why did you choose what you do? Seek ways to challenge yourself again, step outside your comfort zone and take on a new opportunity or two.

What makes you truly happy always comes from within - not from others. It all comes down to what you choose. Step out of indifference. Commit to putting your heart, head and soul into each moment and make the choice to live mindfully.

- With your magic wand, what will you change today?

Your thoughts right now?

"If you think you can or if you think you can't,
either way, you're right."

~Henry Ford~

If I Can Do It, Anybody Can....

All too often we overlook the value of our gifts, talents and skills. We learn from the time we are young to compare and contrast as a way to understand the world. Many times, we judge our worth based on this method. Unfortunately, we often sell ourselves short.

We each have so much to offer each other, yet too often we discount our unique natural gifts (traits). I believe we do this because those natural gifts are so familiar to us that we do not recognize them for the gifts they are.

It's one of those "If I can do it, anybody can," head-scratchers. We tend to overvalue the talents of others, in the "grass-is-always-greener" syndrome, and undervalue our own talents.

Recently, my friends threw me a surprise birthday party. Part of the surprise was a "roast" in which members of the group told little stories and anecdotes about the birthday girl. Most of the attendees know me from different parts of my life, and they have different perspectives and relationships with me. One after another, I heard how our friendship had changed their life and I reflected on how they had enhanced mine. Many of the stories surprised me. I love my friends, and I had no idea that I had such a positive and often humorous effect on others.

The "anybody can do it" syndrome can manifest in so many ways... some can even harm you. Robert is an amazing cartoonist. He enjoys his work, but does not consider his skill unique. No matter the complexity of the character, he charged the same flat fee. He was selling himself short. At my urging, he did some research and became aware that he had unique talents and decided to implement a pricing system based on originality and complexity, instead of the time-for-money system he had been using.

His clients value him more now too. Remember, how you relate to yourself impacts how you relate to the world. Others will not value what's within you if you don't.

- How and where do you discount who you are?

- What gifts do you have that you don't place value on?

Where are you diminishing yourself right now?

"Every moment and every event of every man's life on earth plants something in his soul. For just as the wind carries thousands of winged seeds, so each moment brings with it germs of spiritual vitality that come to rest imperceptibly in the minds and wills of men. Most of these unnumbered seeds perish and are lost, because men are not prepared to receive them: for such seeds as these cannot spring up anywhere except in the good soil of freedom, spontaneity and love."

~Thomas Merton~
— American religious writer & poet,
became a Trappist monk & priest (1915 - 1968)

Be Careful What You Wish For

A friend recently shared with me that she found a letter that she wrote her future self twenty years ago. The letter described in great detail how she wanted her life to be. She'd lost track of the letter, until she found it tucked away in a book. She read it and was amazed that almost all of the items in the letter had manifested in her life.

It's really not that surprising. When you set your unconscious mind on a "problem," it works behind the scenes to solve it, even if you don't keep track of what you told it to do.

Forget about how it will happen, and open the doors to the possibilities that are flooding your life right now. If you have a desire for something, the means to fulfill it are already present, yet it sometimes takes adjusting your viewpoint to see. A mindfulness in action life only asks you to be brave enough to view the world from 360 degrees and face your fears and desires head on.

If you are open to even the most illogical ways they manifest, you will quickly find opportunities abound. (Then the trick is to not be distracted by every bright, shiny object that comes your way.)

Sometimes, what you ask for only comes when you release what you've been tightly holding onto. One Christmas day, I told my sons I was done looking for love. If it happened, it happened. I'd done the work, I knew what I wanted in love, but I was working at it so hard (over 100 blind-dates or warm introduction one-and-dones in one year) that it was impossible for love to come in another way.

It's only when I said, "I'm done..." that the opportunity arose. Who would have ever guessed one-month later to the day I met my beloved in a lobby 1000 miles away from his home and almost 2000 miles away from mine. Always be careful what you ask for — the only problem is that I forgot to ask that he live close by... we are now a bi-coastal couple, as they say.

- What are you asking for?
- Are you stopping yourself from getting it?
- Is there anything stopping you from getting it?

No more apologizing, what do you want right
now?

"An intention is just that, an intention, until you take action... then it becomes real."

~Sharon Sayler~

Pay Attention to the Intention Formula

An intention is defined as a knowing and willing determination or decision to act in a certain way; an act or instance of deciding upon some action or result; resolve. Note that intentions come in all shapes and sizes.

+ WANT (Get clear on what you really want.)

+ CONTROLLED BY YOU (It has to be controlled by you. For example, you do not control wanting someone to quit smoking.)

+ STEPS TO ACHIEVE (How will you get what you want?)

= INTENTION (Set your attention on getting this intention.)

Make sure your intentions are in alignment with your passions, purposes, goals and desires.

For example, let's say, "I want a puppy." Is that controlled by me? It may or may not be. Who else might be involved with the puppy? Take time to consider all those affected by changes that you make. We each have spheres of influence. A sphere of influence is a figure of speech to express how far the effect of someone's power disperses. A sphere of influence can be anyone from our fantasy puppy, to a boss, to an investor... from what mom would think to the voices in your head.

Create a Venn Diagram of all the influences; they can be people, culture(s), physical constraints, etc., and you will see where the competing influences are.

From the view of your Venn Diagram, you can see how even when you set an intention that is controlled by you, things may not go as planned. Consider the new puppy: Will the puppy wreak havoc on your job or other responsibilities? Will others have to change their schedules? If your intention causes a conflict, consider alternatives to your intention before implementation.

As you set your intention(s) realize you can only change (control) yourself. No matter how "good" the intention, it may be misunderstood. There is a saying that goes: "The response you get is the message you sent." The intention behind what you said or did isn't what matters. How your message was received (heard) is what matters.

In this case of the fantasy puppy, let's say it is controlled by me... I then go about figuring out the steps to meeting the perfect puppy.

The "steps to achieve" are the first part of getting our goals. Intentions are easily sabotaged, as an intention is the early formation stage of a goal.

Free Mindful Action Strategy Sheets: Visit www.MindfulnessInActionBook.com for your Attention to your Intention Strategy Sheet.

What are your intentions right now?

"If things are not going well with you, begin your effort at correcting the situation by carefully examining the service you are rendering, and especially the spirit in which you are rendering it."

~Roger Babson~
Statistician and Columnist, 1875-1967

The ABCs of Intentions

The trap of good intentions is that there may be more than one good answer, regardless of your intention. Think of all the "Yeah, but..." and "What if..." times. Ambiguity, beliefs, and contradictions exist everywhere in spite of your desire to be clear on what you want.

The ABCs can be caused by thoughts and feelings that are at odds within you, unresolved emotions, and ignored life lessons, outdated information, etcetera. This internal struggle can be caused by torn loyalties. Often, your friends and family may not want you to change, or maybe they want you to believe the way they do. However clear and positive your intention may be, it can run smack into the well-entrenched beliefs of others. If that happens, practice the following:

Stay calm. Don't take whatever "it" is personally because most often it's not personal.

Listen carefully. Do not interrupt. Use the phrase "Just so I understand..." and repeat their words back as closely as possible to what they expressed.

Reflect on the problem and possible solutions.

Acknowledge and respect why they feel that way. Take it under advisement. Thank them. Take the action you know you need to take.

"Take each day, hour and minute on its own. They are precious and irretrievable."

~ David R. Sanchez~

Everything Expires

I'm all for goal setting, goals serve a useful purpose to give us motivation and a direction. My favorite method for creating a goal is *The Finish Line Goal Formula:*

+ Gotta have it (motivation or intention)

+ Object (stated as a noun)

+ Action (stated as an action verb)

+ Finish Line (stated as a specific Date/Number/Time)

= GOAL

Another acronym that works demonstrates the five attributes of a goal. I used to have only four attributes to a goal, but I think you will agree that the fifth "LEVERAGE" is vital if you are going to get true traction for your success.

Gotta' have it! Be something you want. Say what you want, not what you don't want. If I tell you not to think of a pink elephant, what are you thinking of right now?

Only me. Be under your control. You do not control an intention or goal to get someone to behave differently. It won't work.

Attainable. Be manageable. Split large goals into "baby steps." Suppose you want to earn a million dollars. What would be the step to earning one hundred dollars? One thousand?

Assessable. Be quantifiable, or in some way measurable. As you create each "baby step" toward your goal, give it a date or marker to know when that step is complete. Add sensory-specific "markers" too. What will you see and hear as you achieve each "baby step"? Observing the sensory-specific markers as you achieve each step of your goal is important to keep you on the right path. You can always course-correct.

Leveragable. Is that a word? Leverage is using every "baby step" and what you learn from achieving your goals in multiple ways to get the highest return on your investment of time, energy and money from each goal. Leverage gets you there faster.

Yet, the more we grow, learn and know, the more we change. With change, the things that used to serve us no longer do — they expire. So set your goals as direction and at the same time save space for course correction. In flight school, I learned that if you are just a half-of-degree off on your course as you first take off, you will end up in an entirely different place by the end of the flight due to the law of exponential growth over time. Save space in all goals for course correction as you gather data along the way.

Beware of bright shiny object syndrome (BSO).

What bright shiny object syndrome are taking up space right now?

"The difference between a wish, an intention and a goal is a goal has a definite finish line."

~Sharon Sayler~

A Goal, a BSO or Just Wishful Thinking?

The desire to lead a life of mindfulness can become wishful thinking unless you take specific and measurable action. Leverage creates momentum. Momentum is where the magic happens!

The first action is to define your intention with the previously mentioned intention formula, then plot specific steps toward your goal. At the same time, be open for your goal to appear in another way, shape or form.

Write down the goal in the positive, rather than the negative. Set goals for what you want, rather than what you don't want. For example, "For my current book (my want) I will write (action) my (I control) book (object) on or before October 31, 20__ (specific time)."

I know that sounds a bit crazy — why would you set a goal for something you don't want? Because all to often we don't know what we want, we just know that we don't want "that" anymore. Our environment shapes our goals; if we place ourselves in a negative environment, it is easier to see what we don't want.

To guard against the fear of not taking action for fear it will be the wrong action, plant steps to reevaluate your goal(s) and see if they still work for you or if you are chasing a bright shiny object.

What have you placed in your life that supports you either reaching your goals or not reaching your goals?

Wishing is not a plan and hope won't get it done either! Being specific creates a goal. Write the goal using the verb + noun + date/number = your goal formula. For example, Travel [the action] to Paris [what I want] for Christmas Dec 14, 2014-Jan 4, 2015 [the deadline].

You can always continue to add to your goal as the details become clearer. Set your goal high. Even if you don't make it by the date you wrote in your plan, you are just that much closer....

To paraphrase Dr. Norman Vincent Peale, if you shoot for the moon and hit the stars, it's okay. You've got to shoot for something. A lot of people don't even shoot.

Finally, act upon each of those steps. That's it.

- Think it up.

- Write it down.

- Take action.

Make it real. Remember, momentum is where the magic happens!

Go confidently in the direction of your goals, yet know that the goals can and often do change.

Free Mindful Action Strategy: Visit
www.MindfulnessInActionBook.com
for your Goal Strategy Sheet.

"A winner is someone who recognizes his God-given talents, works his tail off to develop them into skills, and uses these skills to accomplish his goals."

~Larry Bird~

Will You Know Success When You See It?

What is success and how will you know it when you have it? You may have noticed that when people measure their worth only by their external successes, they all too often continue to be disappointed—always needing more.

Could it be that many people don't know the success they are really seeking? Are they actually seeking an "inside job" of success — happiness, peace of mind, a sense of fulfillment, enjoying good friends and family, a purpose – and don't know how to get it?

If you desire to earn a particular salary, is it that you want the cash or the comfort? Whether consciously or not, people usually choose goals based on feelings they attach to those goals, not the actual goals.

Reflect on the goals you wrote down in the "Everything Expires" chapter under *The Finish Line Goal Formula* section of this book.

Be assured that I'm not saying that external rewards of success are wrong. I enjoy the creature comforts like most everyone else. Knowing that the outward symbols of success do not equal how one feels about their own worthiness is the key to living mindfully.

Ask yourself:

- What are my symbols of success?
- What do my symbols of success really mean?
- Why do they matter to me?
- What inner desires and needs do my external symbols/goals represent?
- How will I know success?

What are your thoughts and feelings right now?

"Only if you imagine that the rope is a snake does your heart start pounding. It's your thoughts that scare you into fight-or-flight, not reality."

~Byron Katie~

You Are What You Believe

Beliefs are just beliefs, thoughts are just thoughts. The same thought or belief can serve us as an asset or liability. It just depends on the context and how you choose to act after the thought.

We may not be consciously aware. A belief is something one accepts as true. It may have no basis in truth, yet it is accepted as true. When the belief has little or no basis in truth, it is called a limiting belief.

The problem with a limiting belief is it does just that—it limits us. Think about it as a self-fulfilling prophecy... Here are two examples of positive beliefs:

I can do anything if I set my mind to it.

I deserve the best.

Some readers might say that "I deserve the best," is selfish, or self-centered. Nothing could be further from the truth... this is caring about yourself enough to treat yourself like your best friend. Nobody is with you more than you! A limiting belief often takes the shape of: "I will never get what I want." Remember, before Columbus, the majority knew the world was flat... a belief that was later proven wrong - right?

- What beliefs are rattling around holding you back?

- What beliefs do you hold that are propelling you forward?

"I believe in pink. I believe that laughing is the best calorie burner. I believe in kissing, kissing a lot. I believe in being strong when everything seems to be going wrong. I believe that happy girls are the prettiest girls. I believe that tomorrow is another day and I believe in miracles."

~Audrey Hepburn~

Will You Know Success When You See It?

Maybe we start with a list like Audrey Hepburn's "I believe in pink…". But what else do you believe? Thought viruses and mind gremlins can be lurking in the bumps and folds of your brain… is it the voice of your third-grade teacher, the church-lady, your mom, or maybe a sibling?

"Who cursed your voice?" She asked from across the table.

"Whaaatttt…? Who did what…?" I said with a not-so-subtle mix of surprise and shock.

In that same moment, time slowed down. Scenes from childhood passed before my eyes, as if from a movie; it felt like forever, but when I came back to reality, others of our party were still being seated for dinner.

I'd just met this woman a couple hours earlier at the ICF Conference, where we were both presenting. I kept thinking to myself, "What a crazy thing to say!" I looked at her stunned and speechless. She looked at me in silence.

"My voice cursed? Someone cursed my voice…?" The words kept going through my head, until…. Oh my god, I remembered, the words when my voice had been cursed.

Clear as if it happened yesterday, it was 5th grade, a shy little girl desperate to please— there I was, with five other girls, singing "Danny Boy".

The same "Danny Boy" that had brought Miss Brostoff to tears just 3 months earlier at 4th grade promotion day.

All summer I had been telling myself what a special person I would be when I was selected for Senior Choir. Here I was, the moment of 5th grade choir tryouts had finally arrived.

"Oh Danny boy, the pipes, the pipes are calling...."

Without warning, my 5th grade eyes locked open, stunned, as my worst nightmare was coming true... Miss Brostoff slams down the cover over the piano keys and jumps up, knocking over her stool; she turns, faces me, and with an explosion out comes, "You sing like a dead cow in a bucket! Get out!" One of my worst fears unfolded before me and there was nothing I could do to stop it!

With Miss Brostoff's one comment, I believed so completely that I could not sing - not a note - to the point that I'd never had the courage to sing Happy Birthday (even in a group) to my two sons—both grown men now.

Now, over forty years later, I was reliving it! "Who cursed your voice?" brought back a flood of emotions, thoughts, feelings and beliefs – and not just about singing. In that moment I knew I didn't know if I could sing or not. And I knew I'd allowed someone to hold my voice hostage for decades. This wise woman, Barbara McAfee, gave voice to

110

the truth. My voice had been cursed. Once stated, it no longer had power over me. POOF!

A couple of months later, Barbara and I got together and did a radio show LIVE in her vocal studio in Minneapolis, where I sang (OMG) on air! Yes, that shy, mortified 5th grader sang live, on air, for the first time since she was about eleven. Now, I know I can sing. I'll never be Madonna, Lady Gaga or Maria Callas - but that's not the point.... Until that time I didn't really know if I could or couldn't sing.

Singing with Barbara proved to me once again – you can believe something without knowing it and you can know something without believing it. Most of us know how the latter works. For example, you can know what a politician says, but you don't believe that he means it. However, few take the time to sort out how the former works. Do you know what you believe? That might sound like a simple question, but do you know how and why you believe what you do? Most people carry a lot of beliefs that they just picked up from other people without ever knowing if they are true or not.

Believing and knowing are not the same. Ask a few of your friends what they believe and when they tell you, annoy them by asking, "How do you know that?" They most often will reply with another belief.... And "Bravo!" to the friends that can tell you why they know what they believe. The answers may surprise you!

Ask yourself those same questions.

- What do you believe?
- How do you know that?

Accept the challenge to make a list of what you believe, then next to the belief say how you know it to be true. It's not as easy as it sounds because humans have the amazing ability to engage in coexistence thinking. In other words, we often merge supernatural with natural/ scientific explanations and if recent research from University of Texas at Austin is to be believed (pun intended), we merge them in a "variety of predictable and universal ways."

Do you know why you believe what you do? Or more to the point, do you even know what you believe? It's not until you ask yourself "How do I know that?" about your beliefs that you begin to understand the power — both negative and positive — that beliefs hold over you. An interesting note: Research also suggests that people rarely know how they came to believe what they do, but there are patterns on how we believe something is true or not. The study showed that most often the first step is that we hear something and we believe it, then in a split-second, we begin to compare what we just heard with things we already know and/or believe.

It all happens so fast we rarely realize how we came to our conclusion of whether what we just heard was true or false. When we label something as true or false, it's easy if we have experience or research to back it up. Yet, all too often we let "true" be the default (often taken on blind faith) unless we challenge the messenger for proof. Challenging others is not socially acceptable in most cultures, especially if they hold power of some kind, like your boss. The researchers also discovered a disturbing pattern: if you are distracted during that acceptance and comparison split-second stage, you often don't finish that stage and will accept that statement as true, even if it were one that you would normally reject. Imagine the implications of this one fact, and how easy it is to be manipulated into believing.*

Beliefs can be created when we know something to be true or they can be created when we passively accept information as true. Shocking fact, when you also realize that beliefs play a large part of the operating system of your autopilot of life. If you haven't answered these yet, do it now. The answers may surprise you!

- What do you believe?
- How do you know that?

* Legare, Christine H. The Coexistence of Natural and Supernatural Explanations across Cultures and Development

"Each of us has two ends: one to sit with, and one to think with. Success depends on which one you use; heads you win -- tails you lose."

~Anonymous~
—humor and wisdom appreciated

Clarity Leads to Solid Results

The See it, Say it, Scribble it Formula

Success won't happen unless you make it happen. See it. Say it. Scribble it. Listen to the guiding voice within. Be clear about your intentions and outcomes. Intentionality drives creativity. Creativity drives results. Results drive your goals and successful outcomes.

See it. Stay focused by seeing it. Visualize what you want. Know that focus is not force. Do not force an outcome. Outcomes may arrive differently than we expect. Leave room for the unexpected to amaze and delight you.

Say it. Quit tolerating mediocrity. To attract the results you want, first commit the time and space in your life. Share with others what your goals are, ask for help when needed. Set clear boundaries. If you no longer accept being dragged down by other people's behavior, you'll stop wasting time managing situations that are not yours. The "shoulda, woulda, coulda and what-ifs" of each situation usually revolve around blurred boundaries. Sometimes, we need to let go of situations or things that are not moving us in the direction we want to go in order to make room for what we want and need.

Scribble it. Write it down. Remember that the Finish Line Goal Formula has us put an action verb + a noun(s) + number or date. Writing it down and keeping it in plain sight is a critical piece that is often overlooked. Which takes us back to the "See it" section.... This 3-step process isn't to lock you in or tie you down. It's to make your goal real and become clear on what has to happen. Clarity shows the pathway. You can make your plan simple and flexible even with dates or numbers. That's the easiest way I know to measure your progress.

Get your 3-step Clarity Process action sheet at
www.MindfulnessInActionBook.com

What are you seeking clarity on right now?

"Blessed are the flexible, for they will not be bent out of shape."

~Author unknown~
— humor and wisdom greatly appreciated

Are You Late for Your Life?

Save time to hug your kids. Pay attention to loved ones. Say thank you more often. Breathe! The human bond is more important than the business bond. Family and friends are the ultimate value in life — slow down and ENJOY.

Sometimes, we get going so fast towards what we want, that we forget about the most important parts of our life – our loved ones. It is easy to fall into saying, "Just as soon as..." and know that our loved ones will understand.

A mindful life doesn't work that way. It is the combination of your (work) position and your person. Work-life (position vs. person) balance is not an oxymoron, it's mindfulness in action. Demands on your time change as your family, purposes and work life change. Work-life balance doesn't mean doing everything, nor does it mean everything is equal all the time. It means continually rearranging priorities and appropriate boundaries. Be firm with what you want, as well as what you can and cannot do. Only you can create harmony and happiness in your life.

Research has found that most happy people have strong ties to family and friends and that happy people tend to live longer than unhappy people. Make time for friendships, as it's the strength of our relationships that carry us through life. What's that old truism: "On their deathbed nobody wishes they'd spent more time at the office..."?

"Time is what we want most, but what we use worst."

~William Penn~

Has it Really Been That Long?

Wasting time is worse than wasting money: once spent, it's gone. One day, I walked into my office to find that my assistant, Susan, had put a large poster on the wall—right in front of my desk. "If you don't place any value on your time and work, NO ONE ELSE WILL."

It is still on my office wall today, three desks and six offices later. Susan was never one for subtle. We all need friends like that, the ones who tell you the truth.... You see, when I was just starting out in business, I did not really understand the strength and power behind well-formed intentions and outcomes. I had a business plan that languished in my desk drawer. I didn't know what I really wanted or what I believed other than that I had to pay the bills.

And most importantly, I did not know that you create what you focus on... I stated to everyone that would listen that "I wanted to be busy." That was it. I knew what it meant to me; it meant I wanted clients and work. However, I forgot an important detail... while we got busy fast and my business grew, only my employees were making money. I had just worked myself into a job... when I should have been consciously creating the life I desired.

- What is sucking up all your time?
- What does your extraordinary life look, feel, sound, taste and even smell like?
- What is the first step you will commit to taking in order to get what you just described?

121

"To understand our past mistakes and to neutralize the feelings of shame or guilt over our past inadequacies, we must understand that the acts we commit are neither good nor bad but are only wise or unwise depending upon our particular awareness at that time."

~Thomas D. Willhite~

Four Keys to Knowing When Enough is Enough

Sometimes it's rough to try and stay mindful. Have you ever had thoughts like these?

You love what you're doing, but you can't make a living at it or it's taking too much time away from family.

You are in a bad relationship and you know it, but it's just so much easier to stay with what you know.

You really want to go back to school, make a change, travel somewhere, but you don't because someone else disapproves.

Time to do some homework – maybe they are right or maybe they are wrong. But you won't know if there is a more mindful way of fulfilling your desires unless you spend some time to:

Recognize the real need(s) within the dilemma. Often people will stick to their illusions until something forces them to recognize their misperceptions. All progress depends on recognizing what is real and what is not real. Gain freedom from ambiguity and list the real needs.

For example, Deb is a spendthrift and her husband Doug is a spender. They fight about money "all the time" as she tells it.

They both earn a good living and are very comfortable by most standards, yet they still fight about money. Why?

Because neither understands the real need of the other. Once the real needs are uncovered, solutions become easy. Through a process called nonviolent communication created by Dr. Marshall Rosenberg it becomes easy to hear our own deeper needs and those of others. * Deb's real need was in having "enough money as a safety net." A money cushion made her feel safe. Doug on the other hand needed to be needed; it was important to him to give people what they wanted or needed. Once they realized each other's deep needs it became easier to accept and to compromise.

Accept. Once recognized, accept the situation, warts and all. This isn't a time to judge yourself or others harshly or label yourself a failure. It's time to give yourself grace that you will do better next time because of the lessons you have learned this time. Acknowledge and accept the need(s).

Determine. It can be uncomfortable to determine what must change. Openly share with trusted allies AND know that no one else can or should do it for you. People will change (including ourselves!), you just have to overcome a little bit of resistance. Openly and candidly share what you would like to have happen next. This can feel very vulnerable, so have everyone involved share ground rules such as: it's okay to share what we are observing, what emotions we are feeling, the values we want to live by, and what we want to ask of ourselves and others. This isn't the time to use the language of blame, judgment or domination.

Act. Take direct mindful action. Commit to doing what it takes, even if it is quit and try something else. It always gives me joy when I experience the deep pleasure of contributing to my own and others' well-being.

- What is your enough?
- Where is your enough?

This four-step process sounds simple, but it's not always easy. It might not work at first, but as long as you face reality head-on, each attempt will give insights, better understanding and ultimately the right solution.

- Be open.
- Be present.
- Breathe!

* http://www.cnvc.org/about/marshall-rosenberg.html

"There are two things to aim at in life: first, to get what you want, and after that, to enjoy it. Only the wisest of mankind achieve the second."

~Logan Pearsall Smith~

I Did What?!

Right now, grab and pen and off the top of your head, write five things in your life you wish you had done differently or had done better. This isn't about creating a regret list; it's about understanding the chorus in the unconscious mind.

Are there conflicting parts of you telling you a whole Pandora's box of forgotten crud?

Are there similarities (patterns) to these five events?

What patterns are you allowing to run your life and diminish your passion and purposes?

Now, list twenty-five accomplishments in your life that <u>you are most proud of</u>. I know from experience this isn't as easy than it sounds. Our mind files away our successes with a wonderful label of DONE! We've resolved whatever it was, so no need to keep it front and center anymore. You probably found it easier to do the "Do Differently" list, but please no judgment here; this list could be anything from surviving a scary time in your life, to saving a kitten stuck in a tree, to learning to swim, to passing the spelling test, to getting the Nobel prize...

Read the list of 25 aloud and give yourself a round of applause!

Compare the five with the twenty-five. Most likely they all unlocked access to parts of yourself that you may not have even been aware of.

- As you went through this experiment, was it your head-chorus or your mindful actions that were in control of it?

- Did you find yourself struggling to come up with successes?

- Did you have feelings of unworthiness or excitement?

Your thoughts right now?

"Every time Elaine and I go into a wine shop, she picks up this one opener and swears it was her idea... I love to bug her with my belief that the same idea is given to a certain number of people all at the same time and the one who acts on it first wins!"

~Sharon Sayler~

Step Into Your Dream Now

Now, glance back at the "I did what?" list of five things you wish had gone better—what did you learn from each one and how has that lesson helped you? With those insights and lessons, think back to a time of a great idea or a desired grand adventure or dream job you didn't do....

- What is it?

- Why didn't you do your big idea, grand adventure, or your dream?

- Examine your "why." Is that "why" really true? Is the "why" yours or someone else's?

- Are you now, or did you then tell yourself something to stop you or hear something that stopped you? Is it your voice or someone else's?

- If you choose now to revive that passion or dream, what would it take?

"True friends are those who lift you up when your heart's wings forget how to fly."

~Author unknown~
— wisdom greatly appreciated

Have the Courage to Share

Success sometimes requires the courage to risk disapproval. I know as I write this book and share my personal foibles and struggles, it's again opening myself up to critics. I also know that I've surrounded myself over the years with great mentors and teachers and have spent my lifetime learning what I write about today. I'm blessed to have people in my world who "have my back" and I choose to surround myself with those that support my work and love me for me -including the foibles.

When I wrote *What Your Body Says and How To Master The Message,* it was the biggest launch of one my books at that time. I had numerous well-known authors, celebrities and self-help gurus helping me spread the word about the book. It also opened up the world of critics on a more massive scale. I'd been coached and counseled by my friends of what to expect, yet nothing really prepares you for silly "feedback."

I know I've got big-girl-britches for true feedback and debate, but two days after the book came out I got an email along with a twitter rant and Facebook postings that I had "girthy arms" and my hair was "too long for my age to be a body language expert...." Crazy but true, a woman decided she had to spread the word that my girthy arms (which I still don't know what those are as I'm really of rather small frame) disqualified me to be a body language expert! Of course, I haven't been dissuaded from my message. Iyanla Vanzant shares, "The only thing that goes on in your life is what you allow to go on in your life." Don't be dissuaded.

Just fasten your seatbelt and go forth with what you are meant to do as you will always hit some bumps and have a few twists and turns along the way.

- In what ways can you share your knowledge, encourage and support others?

Your thoughts right now?

"We are all connected, when you uplift and support one, you support the whole."

~Sharon Sayler~

Got Your Back, Jack!

Think about those people who will support you when you share your intentions, goals, passions and desires with them. Support can be anything from encouragement to sharing knowledge to quality feedback.

Just like feedback, know that not all support is created equal. I have a great, long-time friend. She wants to always be loving and supportive, however at times, she will not tell me what I need to hear. From her love and kindness, she tells me what she thinks I want to hear, not what I may need to hear. Want-to-hear and need-to-hear are not always the same and although the truth may sting for a moment, know that in that short-lived sting of self growth— like the proverbial "Do these pants make me look fat?" question, the answer may not be what you want, but at least you know what others are thinking.

For example, a woman we will call Meg came to me and asked, "Why does everyone always say I'm judging them?" After some exploration it became obvious why most people would label her facial expressions as "judgmental" or "critical". But what kind of feedback is "stop being so judgmental"?

Meg, a person highly committed to systems and processes, wasn't judging. She was trying to be helpful and had immediately gone "inside" to start her step-by-step how-to list to solve your problem

137

that "systems people" just have to do.   For example: When I asked Meg, "How do you make soup?" Immediately her eyes narrowed and her brows furrowed. Her lips squeezed together and her eyes went blank... she'd gone "inside" to find the answer. When I showed her a picture of "her face making that face" she agreed, that face looked judgmental.

Now she understood why her boss constantly accused her of "doing it" just to annoy him. When she saw "that face" she knew what "it" was. Yet, the high need for systems and processes are part of who she is. It would be difficult to change and not necessary.

Our work around was two-fold: first, carry a pad of paper and pen and write out the request and the steps. This will keep her focus external and she doesn't make "that" face while she is writing notes. Second, tell her boss, coworkers, friends and family she makes that face when she's solving problems and that it's not personal to them. She did both. She called me a day later and said that I "saved" both her job and her marriage. I didn't even know she was married, but she ran home from our session, told her husband, "Sharon says I make this face when I'm thinking." They both laughed as he said, "I thought you had hated every idea I ever had!"

Seek counsel from those who will give you honest feedback. The feedback may or may not work for you, but at least you will have another way of looking at something.

Try to approach the comments from the other person's point of view. Hold the "Yeah, buts" and the "That will never work...."

Even if the feedback is tough to hear, ALWAYS graciously thank them for their courage to share their thoughts and opinions.

- Who in your world has your back?
- How do you return their support?

"We don't see things as they are, we see them as we are."

~Anais Nin~

It's Not Personal

Understand that nay-sayers, critics and alike have their own illusions about reality, just like those around Meg thought her facial expression was all about them being judged. As you saw, it wasn't personal to those seeing the expression! It's just Meg!

Know that we each have our own reality. Who in your world discourages you? Think about one person who told you, "You can't do that," or "your idea is crazy." Now think about the things you accomplished because of that comment. Did you finish something because they said you couldn't? Or perhaps you decided never to treat others that way. Even the nay-sayers can be a grateful gift. It's the challenges that make the successes so much sweeter.

Maybe the nay-sayer is not outside of us. Most of us have a chorus in our heads chanting to us constantly, telling us how to feel, what to believe, what to do and not do. Maybe the voices aren't even yours...what if they were from a critical parent or childhood teacher?

You have the choice to quiet the chorus and change or stay the same. Even not making a choice is a choice. It takes courage and heart to take bold steps to release the hold this chorus has on thoughts and feelings.

"...Internal joy comes from within, external joy comes and goes with whatever is happening in our environment."

~James Kitchens~
— author of *Talking to Ducks*

The Asset of Anger

Do critics, bullies and nay-sayers make you angry?

Anger is a secondary emotion. To get angry, typically, you have been hurt, frustrated or frightened first. When you realize you are angry, think back to your choice to get angry... which were you: hurt, frightened, or frustrated? Was it your ego that was hurt? There is a big difference between being hurt physically compared to offending your ego, which may be fragile.

Once you determine the base cause, you have a choice to change how you think and feel about the situation. Thoughts and feelings are not the real you. They are not facts. Yet, all too often, they are the basis for your choices, usually based on patterns built and used over time — that may or may not work for you anymore.

When you feel yourself getting angry next time, critically assess your position and all likely outcomes before choosing what to do next. The five questions to ask yourself are:

- Is this a fight worth fighting? What other options do I have, such as thanking them for their opinion and moving on?

- Do I have enough information, history, etc.? Maybe I don't understand where the nay-saying is coming from. It often is the other person's personal fears being expressed as if they were your fears.

143

- Does this involve me personally or am I fighting someone else's battle?

- What are the possible outcomes? Could I be fired, demoted, lose pay, or lose a friend?

- Am I hurt, frightened or frustrated? Can I stay dispassionately involved? Is this my ego wanting to fight?

If you feel you have to move forward and address what may become a conflict, then first determine the volatility of the participants and the situation. Personal safety is number one; request professional help when necessary. Once personal safety is assured, and you have answered the above questions, explore these seven possible causes of the critics, bullies and nay-saying:

- Diverse needs, wants and desires

- Different personality styles

- Conflicting perceptions or expectations of the situation

- Dissimilar goals

- Outside pressures or competing spheres of influence

- Differing personal values or views of fairness and power

- Unpredictable policies from leadership or management

While it is important to consider what the root of the nay-saying / conflict may be, it is surprisingly easy to get caught up in the back-story and get even more riled up. Work to remain a neutral observer, even though you are part of the actual problem. If time permits, gather specific, verifiable data and information.

From the neutral observer position, step back into the present and look at the situation. With curiosity, look back at yourself, over there, and ask if the events that led you to become hurt, frustrated, and/or frightened were true. If they are true, really true, thank yourself for paying attention.

Stay angry if you must and set an intention to resolve the situation. We often hold back making changes, or truth telling for fear of "hurting" another person when the worst that might happen is that their ego is offended.

Be willing to be offended and speak your truth, knowing that we cannot truly hurt another unless you intend to — and perhaps the other party intends to... either way, if they are true or they are not true, apply liberal doses of appreciation for the chance to open your eyes to something new.

"Reward the negative with attention, you get more negative. Reward the positive with attention, you get more positive."

~Source unknown~
—but greatly appreciated

Reward Your Positives

Instead of focusing on the negative, build the habit of rewarding the positive. At the end of every day, write down your successes and the successes of those you love and care about.

Gail gathers family successes all year by writing them on colorful paper and saving them in a special box. At Christmas she has family members read them aloud to those gathered around the table. Each success is celebrated again. It is a wonderful way to remind family and friends of the passions and joys in living.

Another friend of mine, Deedee, has a different spin on the same idea. She started trying to actively focus on the positive in her life, and decided to make a conscious effort to recognize moments that were special. Whether those were moments of success, moments of joy, or moments of love, she wrote them all down and put them into a jar that she had decorated with the quote, "Collect moments, not things." Some of those moments were written on brightly colored paper, while others were written on napkins or receipts from the places that the moments occurred— because after all, uplifting moments can happen anywhere! On New Year's Eve, she opens them all and reflects on how amazing her year has been. Just the act of recognizing each positive moment instills gratitude in everyday life, as well as a positive attitude. You can't look at a jar filled with happy memories and not smile a bit to yourself at everything positive that you've experienced.

Keep a Success or Gratitude Journal. It is often easy to forget the positive and dwell on the negative. Typically we focus on the negative because it needs fixing. The positive does not need the extra focus, so it is easy to dismiss and move onto the next "problem."

If you are a journaler, an amazing tip I learned years ago is to journal only on the right side of the pages first. Then at a set time later, whether it is one month, six months or a year, go back to re-read what you wrote on the right-side pages. On the left-side pages now write what's changed. It's a marvelous way of seeing in writing that ancient Persian Sufi poet's wisdom of "This too shall pass."

Make a habit of focusing on the positive—there is positive in every situation. Praise works miracles.

- Who can you praise today?

Free Mindful Action Strategy: Visit www.MindfulnessInActionBook.com for your Success Journal, Gratitude Journal and Success Sheets.

Your thoughts right now?

"Progress is impossible without change, and those who cannot change their minds cannot change anything."

~George Bernard Shaw~

You Are a Work in Progress

Removing what you do not like does not mean that what you DO like will automatically appear. Things do not always go as planned.

Sometimes, things just do not feel right. Honor those feelings. We may feel we are leading a life beside ourselves, or that we are in our own way... Honor those feelings by examining what happened just prior to those feelings. Like a video tape, rewind and rerun what just happened.

Is it a pattern of behavior you repeat often?

Is it congruent with the person you want to be?

Edit those moments when you wish things had gone differently. Edit in the third person and program your success in the first person. For example: "That person, over there [point to a specific location] did XYZ. I would never do that! If I were to be in the same situation, I would do ABC!" Editing behavior in the third person doesn't apply the "I am..." label to yourself and programming in the first person programs you to do the behavior you are now wanting quickly and easily.

Imagine for a moment that you are walking beside yourself. Looking back at the "you" over there, take a moment to notice what the "you" over there is doing right now.

- Would you choose to be the person you see over there?

"Choose carefully. You are a mirror for others and they for you. When you reflect happiness, you will see happiness."

~Sharon Sayler~

It's Always a Choice

Living a mindful life is a life by choice. Having an amazing life, a passionate life, an aware life isn't chance, karma, or even kismet. It's a choice. You have the power to choose to be resentful, heartsick, burdened, dissatisfied, full of worry and anxiety, to be calm, satisfied, happy, and to be passionate.

The thoughts you choose to dwell on move you through time. Resentment, guilt and being heartsick are emotions of the past. Worry and anxiety are about the future. Now is calm, satisfied, happy, and passionate. Moving through the now — moment-to-moment — keeps the feelings of the past and future at bay.

Practicing joy, mindfulness and passion for and in the present moment is a release—a relief from forecasting in fear or frustration and reflecting with regret.

Future pacing and reflection on the past are tools. They help answer our current questions and allow us to ask better questions next time. Future pacing and reflection allow us to learn. The key to mindful living is to choose without placing the emphasis on what you "should" do, or what you "should have done" in the past.

"Losers live in the past. Winners learn from the past and enjoy working in the present toward the future."

~Denis Waitley~

Accept the Past, It's Gone

Get out of your head and into your life. We cannot change what happened. If you owe apologies – give them. If you owe gratitude – express it.

Look forward to a better tomorrow, while allowing yourself to fully experience the present. We show others who we are in many ways. Regardless of what we say, our body language and the energy we project will give away our true state of being.

So often I hear, "I had no choice." This is not so. Even by choosing not to make a choice, you just made the choice of inaction.

A client, Mary, tells me that she must learn everything the hard way. When asked, "How come?" she just shrugs her shoulders. Notice the all-or-nothing thinking of the word "must." When you hear *must, should, never* and *always*, it is a sign of all-or-nothing thinking.

Very few things in life are absolute. Taking single events and using them to make wider generalizations is counter-productive. Each single event involves unique choices. Every choice you make moves you closer to or farther away from your goals.

- Where are you stuck in all or never thinking?

"If you realized how powerful your thoughts are, you would never think a negative thought."

~Peace Pilgrim~

—Teacher / spiritual leader 1908-1981

Abandon Negative Attachments

Building the life you love can, at times, feel like one step forward, two steps back. Fear, resistance, and even guilt will emerge in the strangest places and times. These emotions are usually attached to the past—unresolved feelings, outdated beliefs and ignored, yet repeated, unlearned lessons. What are you afraid of admitting even to yourself?

Sadly, many people let fear hold them back from even beginning, let alone mindfully living, life. Many are content to sit on the sidelines and complain. Another group plays only a part of the game, never trying too much. Fear comes up with reasons to stay within a comfort zone that seem reasonable. These reasons work at some level; they keep us safe.

Now, I'm not talking about rational fear. Stepping in front of a moving bus is a rational, reasonable fear. The types of fear that stop mindful, passionate living are the ones locking you to the past.

- What is holding you back?
- What would happen if you let go?

"It's not what happens in your life, it's what you make with what happens that matters."

~Source unknown~
— but greatly appreciated

Perfection Paralysis

I have a confession to make: I am a recovering perfectionist... That perfectionism crippled me, paralyzed me from taking action. If I wasn't sure that an idea was absolutely foolproof, perfect, and no one could ever see fault in it, I didn't want to share what I could offer the world. I have wanted to write about this topic for some time, but could not for several reasons. I am not a counselor; I am not an expert on the human condition. But, I have learned a few things along the way and have the passion to share what I have learned the hard way in hopes of easing your journey.

As I work through my own perfection paralysis, I have learned that part of perfection paralysis is fear: fear of the unknown, fear of not being good enough, fear of being judged, or worse, fear of being too good... "Oh, no, what if I'm as successful as I know I can be?" Just to name a few....

- Is fear part of your desire for perfection?
- What have you been meaning to get done?
- What do you need in order to do it?

"Indecision is the seedling of fear."

~Napoleon Hill~

Are You Frozen in Time?

Alice knew she had to make a decision, but she seemed frozen. The deadline was looming, yet she was stuck pondering all the reasons how to do and why she couldn't do the project — the biggest one of her career.

In reality, she could have done it in a number of ways if she had chosen to. She had the skills and knowledge to do the project, yet she could not make a decision, so the deadline came and went and she lost the project! She later rationalized that it really wasn't the right project for her, yet she was over the moon when she got the news she'd been awarded the project. What happened? She got stuck in her "what ifs," and her "what abouts."

The Hindu philosopher Shankaracharya writes that even great warriors, in the midst of the battle, have a fearful body and mind, but their spirit is fearless.

Breathe in, breathe out, on each exhale detach from your "what if" thoughts that are keeping you stuck. Reach out for support.

Decision-making techniques are numerous. The most common for straight-forward decisions is to simply list pros and cons or talk to friends and family. My favorite when making an important choice is a SWOC analysis (strengths, weaknesses, opportunities and challenges). For more complex decisions, consider the Rational Decision 8-Step Process.

First, clearly identify the problem or question. Then determine what are the major objectives you are to accomplish, and look for all alternative ways to achieve those objectives.

Evaluate the alternatives for who, what, when, where, how and how much (for money, time, etc.) Select the alternative most likely to succeed— balancing your fears of what can go wrong versus what can go right.

Break down that alternative into the steps you need to complete. It is often easiest to work backwards, starting at the desired outcome and saying "What was the step that I completed just before I succeeded? And before that, I did...?" As you begin to implement, track your progress by collecting data and measurements to know you are on the correct track? It's easier to course correct early on. As you achieve your goal, be sure and celebrate your success.

Whatever decision-making technique works for you, use it!

Log-on to www.MindfulnessInActionBook.com to get your Decision-Making worksheet samples

Where are you stopping yourself right now?

"The road to success is lined with many tempting parking spaces."

~Source Unknown~

The FEAR Family: FEAR, and Its Friends, "Resistance" and "Guilt"

Jerry Seinfeld shared, "At a funeral, most people would rather be in the casket than giving the eulogy." Too true! That's fear, yet most people say things like, "Oh, I'm not a good public speaker," or "I wouldn't know what to say…". That's Fear talking….

I've had clients that know certain suggestions I make would make a difference, yet they steadfastly say, "Come up with a different answer, because I don't like that." It could be as simple as write an email or make a phone call…yet some fear, from somewhere, is keeping them from moving towards what they say they want. That's resistance sharing the mind-stage with fear….

Then they complain and blame all types of events, people and situations for not getting what they set out to get. Many even have a "If only I had done…" mind-battle when the moment has past. That's guilt now pushing fear and resistance off the mind-stage. Guilt can be a drama queen and often likes to stick around on the mind-stage far too long.

Consider the four most common fears that stop us from reaching our full potential:

F: Failure

E: Embarrassment

A: Awesomeness

R: Rejection

These fears are based in not knowing what will happen next just like most fears. It's a fear of leaving what you know for what you don't know. That's where the axiom for fear as "false evidence appearing real" comes from. I like it, but sometimes the evidence is real or we don't recognize what we are feeling as fear.

Not knowing is never fun, but thinking we know what's going to happen next is really a construct of our mind. Do we really truly know what will happen next? No, we only know what will probably happen next based on what has happen previously. Those moments of not knowing can often feel like a free-fall. It can be uncomfortable. Yet, I haven't found a way to make great strides in getting what you want without those moments of having to consciously breathe fully and completely, then trusting, just trusting you will know what to do when the time comes.

Living courageously, consciously and mindfully requires us to acknowledge that many parts of us exist including fear, resistance and guilt. This trio is part of our internal safety gatekeepers.

Managing the mental side of the FEAR family is a life-long commitment and being mindful of your triggers and where you resist growth and change will allow you to consciously take control to break through those fears that appear very real.

Don't let these hidden fears of greatness keep you from your full potential.

- Where are you shoving a brick under your own success accelerator...?

- What fears do you allow to stand in your way?

"Grace — the outward manifestation of a mindful soul."

~Sharon Sayler~

The Power of Grace

One of the biggest lessons I have learned and one of the hardest to implement over the years is how important it is to give yourself and others grace. The word "grace" has several meanings. I prefer, "the disposition to be generous or helpful, to bestow goodwill." You are in control. Renew your courage with grace. Give yourself the same grace, respect and permission to mess up that you would give your dearest friend.

Give yourself and others:

Grace when you are wrong

Grace when you are right

Grace when things don't go your way

Grace when they do

Grace to freely explore interests and passions

Grace to say "Yes"

Grace to say "No"

Grace to say "Thank you"

Grace to say "I love you"

- Is it time to change the way you think and speak about yourself?

- What would you see differently if you revitalized your awareness and life with grace?

"Remember that not getting what you want is sometimes a wonderful stroke of luck."

~Dalai Lama~

Getting What You Want

As a child, I used to play the game of Hearts with my beloved Aunt Myrtle. Hearts makes you create a strategy from what you are dealt. The rules of the game give the best planners and strategists an edge. Even if one round goes badly, the game keeps going, round after round. The strategy to Hearts is to get others to play their cards the way you want them to. Even the worst hand can end up winning with the right plan.

Life teaches us this every single day. Life is filled with compelling choices and equally compelling consequences. Life is one game where you define your rules. You can always start again and even choose the quitting time.

The only way to lose is not to play. You may lose a round or two, as things don't always work out as planned—yet as a firm believer that everything happens for a reason, I believe we sometimes have to look at events from more than a glass-half-full or half-empty perspective.

- You have "a glass" — what are you going to do with it?

"Living in a crisis-du-jour world may bring you attention, but is it the type of attention you really want?"

~Sharon Sayler~

Note: For real victims who are struggling to overcome, recover, and move beyond true trauma, I am in no way taking aim at you. Wishing you all the blessings, grace and guidance you need to exceed at what you desire and dream to do.

Are You Living a Crisis-du-jour?

Let's face it: there is no shortage of "professional victims." Perhaps you know someone that lives life with a crisis-du-jour. Often, these individuals are in a lose-lose frame of mind.

Perpetual victimhood can be addictive, gives momentary pleasure, hinders the exploration of reality and destroys quality relationships. A "professional victim," as we see in the media, has advantages:

- You are not responsible for what happened to you — of course, past choices have no bearing.

- You are not accountable to anyone for anything.

- You are entitled to understanding and empathy.

- You are justified in your moral indignation for being wronged (or caught).

As you can see, these are amazing privileges. Be aware that perpetual victimhood can be contagious too. I met this guy, we will call him "Fred," through a training I attended. While we didn't see a romantic relationship as possible, we enjoyed some of the same things. Pretty soon, we were meeting every Thursday for happy hour at a local place just to catch up and talk about life. At first, I ignored his comments about the bad service or the poor quality of food, or the bad thing that had happened

173

at work or the way he'd been wronged by a mutual friend and the list goes on and on....

But then one day, another friend said, "What's wrong with you, Sharon? You used to be so positive. It's like your life is going to hell in a handbasket!" Wow, that was a real wake-up call. It got me wondering what was wrong with me — things were going poorly, but not that poorly! Thursday night rolled around and I'm still in that wondering frame of mind when I started to hear the "everything is wrong" routine from Fred. Snap went the mental puzzle piece! I'd caught "professional victim-itis!"

- Have you ever caught "professional victim-itis?"

Explore what happened – be mindful of catching it again. It is highly contagious and very dangerous to the health and well-being of yourself and those you love.

What are your feelings and thoughts right now?

"Learn to make most of your expectations into preferences - it's easier."

~Michael Grinder~

The Problem with Expectations and Preferences

At times, we have expectations of how things should be. Expectations are the needs, wants, and preconceived ideas we have of how things should be. They come from our beliefs, thoughts and feelings. Know that they are just that: beliefs, thoughts and feelings. They are not you and they can change.

Make a conscious choice about your expectations. Sometimes, we do need a true expectation, that's okay. For example, I expect my doctor to be competent and well-trained.

Choose those expectations that are really preferences and let them go. Give others the benefit of the doubt; all too often we take things personally and in my experience, 99% of the time they aren't! There is a big problem with unrealistic expectations. One I hear from women about the men in their lives is "He should have known!" My answer is "maybe, maybe not - does he read minds?"

See, with many expectations, if "he" did behave the way you wanted, then it's not a problem... If an expectation is met, then satisfaction is the result. You "win." Yet, when you fight a battle you don't need to, or shouldn't, even if you win, you lose. Pick your battles or you can get into all sorts of sticky problems with your expectations about other people.

- We know that we cannot control others, yet many times we are disappointed when they don't meet our expectations. Why?

- "I would prefer 'X' behave this way," relieves you of the need to control others. Do you really need to win 'em all?

- Do you have unrealistic expectations of others?

- What expectations in your life do you need to change into preferences?

Note: Sometimes people do have burdens too big to bear, and sometimes they just think they do. They may need our strength, time or knowledge. Good boundaries support and encourage others without carrying them.

Your thoughts right now?

"Self-image sets an individual's boundaries."
~Sharon Sayler~

What's Yours? What's Mine?

Having clear boundaries is essential to a mindful, balanced life. Boundaries are most often related to your self-concept and self-worth. Boundary-setting abilities vary; many are good at setting boundaries with certain people, yet cannot set boundaries with others.

People with boundary-setting problems have distorted views about control and responsibility. Setting boundaries can produce feelings of guilt and emotional debt. Sometimes people with blurred boundaries feel:

- It is mean to hold people responsible for their choices and behaviors

- The other person will not make the right choice

Boundaries with limiting beliefs can cause people to lose track of what belongs to them and what belongs to other people, which leads to the need to resort to controlling behavior. Experience your consequences and let others experience theirs. Ask yourself:

- What is mine? What parts are mine?

- What is theirs? What parts are theirs?

- How and why do I feed this situation?

- What is my secondary gain in maintaining blurred boundaries?

- What will I do instead?

"The weak can never forgive. Forgiveness is the attribute of the strong."

~Mohandas Karamchand Gandhi~

Forgiveness is for You

Norman Cousins once said, "Life is an adventure in forgiveness." These are some of the truest words I've heard. We each have something or someone to forgive. Life is in constant motion. No matter how hard you try to stay in the moment, there will be situations that test you.

Respect your boundaries. Learn from what happened. You have no control over what anyone else feels or thinks or does. No matter how hard we try, sometimes people will just do what they are going to do!

When there's mutual respect, "working things through" can heal. If you feel threatened, withdrawal from the situation may be a viable option. Be honorable and intend the best for everyone, including yourself, even if that means that you choose to move forward without them. That's okay, if that's what you need to do.

Bless them for the time you shared and the positive you've learned. Sometimes people come into your life for a reason and when that reason is complete, it's time to bless and move on. Only when you're at peace can you make a real contribution to anyone. If you are holding on tightly to grudges, there is little space left to help others who truly deserve it. Blessing is not forgetting, it's forgiving, and forgiving is for you.

There is an old saying I heard years ago, that holding tightly to an offense, no matter how heinous it was, is like feeding yourself poison and waiting for the other person to die. It just doesn't work.

How do you feel right now?

"He who trims himself to suit everyone will soon whittle himself away."

~Raymond Hull~

What Will the Neighbors Say?

Do you follow your rules or society's rules for what you should be? Back when I graduated from high school, young ladies were expected to be one of three things: a wife, nurse, or elementary teacher while waiting to become a wife.

This may sound harsh, but society is not concerned with you. Society is concerned with keeping society stable. Society is not concerned that you should live a mindful, passion-filled life. It is concerned that you become an effective, efficient and compliant part of society. To do this, it attempts to mold you with labels, so that you won't become a problem to it.

The most effective weapon for society is your ego. Society does its best to give you an ego that fits within its needs. Ethics, morality, what we want others to think of us, and laws are all good mechanisms, but society also labels a person to keep them "in their place." If you believe that label, then there you are - stuck and most likely unhappy with no idea why!

Remember, your limiting beliefs are sometimes so implanted that the roots go deep and wide to keep you "in the place you belong." I would not be a writer now had I listened to society or my mom.

Pick your battles well, for some can be better fought with silence then defiance. Opinions, passions, purposes and preferences all differ. Give others the benefit of the doubt, the same as you hope they do for you. We can never really know what another wants, needs or feels.

- Whose permission are you waiting for?

What would the neighbors say right now?

"I am not myself. I am the potential of myself."
~Anna Deavere Smith~

The Accumulated Ego

I know I just railed on ego the previous chapter with "The most effective weapon for society is your ego.... Yet, it plays an important role as one of the gatekeepers to your inner self. It sorts information and provides feedback, both positive and negative to your feelings of self-worth and self-confidence.

Ego listens to others and accumulates "the stereotype labels" for yourself and others. Acknowledge and appreciate the job that ego does, however, know that labeling others is the lazy man's shorthand for getting to know someone.

Ideally, your ego is aware of itself and the world around it and will not allow falsehoods to enter, but often ego fails us too. It can trap us with long accumulated beliefs and outdated information that it still believes to be true. It takes mindful action to control ego and not let ego control you:

Be willing to look beyond the negative labels that ego has accumulated and examine the "why" of your thoughts, emotions, beliefs, passion(s) and purpose(s). Unfortunately, ego often takes the path of least resistance and accepts your and others' labels (judgments) of yourself as true. Mindfully choose new ways of talking to and about yourself and the world will follow.

Break free of your labels and those you apply to others. Consider using the "Isn't that interesting, I wonder what that's about?" label if you must label. Living without labels for yourself and others is not an overnight event though - give yourself grace here.

Labels are the shorthand you use to file items away in your memory. It's how you sort and quickly categorize for your memory. Labeling allows you to quickly assess a situation and say, "Oh, it looks like 'X' and 'Y' worked last time so I'll try 'Y' this time...."

An ego full of feelings of unworthiness and self-doubt is created through fear of loss, fear of separation and/or "I'm the center-of-the-universe" thinking. By staying in the now and mindfully looking to the positive, your negative labeling habit will die from lack of energy. But stay aware, those labels are lurking out there everywhere, just waiting to attach their tentacles to you again!

- What are your favorite labels and what will you do instead, now?

Your thoughts right now?

"If you don't know where you are going, what does it matter which road you take?"

~Cheshire Cat to Alice, facing a fork in the road~

Choose Your Life.

Approach your passions, purposes and life with consideration and curiosity....

Choose your life mindfully. It's the best choice you will ever make.

Take action on those choices.

Accept yourself exactly as you are, where you are now. Know that you will grow and change – ever-evolving into who you want to be.

Open your mind before jumping into action.

The "quick-fix" is never quick. When it is painful, we tend to want it over quickly. Be willing to allow all possibilities. It's okay to give the unexpected a chance.

Banish negative self-talk. Labels and thoughts such as "I'll never be able to do it!" or "This is impossible!" stop the subconscious mind from searching for solutions. Reframe the negative self-talk into questions of curiosity. "How can I do this?" or "How is this possible?" The phrase, "Where can I find out how to...?" releases the imagination to discover new ideas.

Have courage, put your heart out into the world and your mind into action. Make room for the magic of the unexpected. Remember, momentum is where the magic happens!

"Accept what you've created and allow space to always re-create."

~Sharon Sayler~

Re-Creation

We are the only species that can choose to be any way we would like to be. We can manifest our intentions and recreate ourselves. Many times in life, I have had to make choices that recreated who I was. Each recreation released new insights into my Self, showing me new passions and purposes, strengths and weaknesses. It opens up new doors and presents new opportunities too.

Re-Creation can take many forms. After each joyous birth of my sons—suddenly, I was recreated; first as Mom and then as Mom of two! Or, through a painful divorce after twenty-three years of marriage, I was again recreated as a single mom, and now, an empty nester and new grandmother. These experiences have given me a deeper understanding of passions and purposes and how some change and others stay the same throughout your life.

It is in how mindfully aware you choose to be, that your passions emerge and your purposes are revealed. It is each context of your life that defines its unique purpose. It is that which brings you joy in each context of your life that creates a mindful, passionate life. Only you have that answer.

- What are those answers for right now?

"The life I touch for good or ill will touch another life, and that in turn another, until who knows where the trembling stops or in what far place my touch will be felt."

~Frederick Buechner~

Interconnections

Things can be more complex than they seem. How often have you noticed that when you go to improve one thing, you find it's connected to everything else? Just ask anybody who has ever started a remodeling job! I recently wanted to add a shower to my guest bath. As the floor was being prepped, I heard those words no one wants to hear: "Uh-oh." The contractor had noticed dry rot. Removing the dry rot showed the need for a new floor joist that evolved into a new floor and floor covering, that meant the cabinet needed to be removed, and while it was out I notice how well-worn it was looking so I replaced it too.... This job took a month longer and many more dollars than expected—all I wanted was a shower, but I got a whole new bathroom.

As you notice interconnections, consider giving yourself some time, space and grace instead of giving yourself the third degree. Be gentle with yourself and others. Just like ripples in a pond, as one area changes all the other areas change as well. You may notice family and friends act differently as they respond to your changes and new way of being. It's just the cycle of growth, when a new seed grows some dirt has to give way... It's all good!

- What seeds of change will you mindfully plant today?

- What is your intention for those seeds?

- How will you nurture their growth?

"If you take responsibility for yourself you will develop a hunger to accomplish your dreams."

~Les Brown~

Stretch Your Mind, Awareness and Imagination

Attitude affects achievement. Have you ever met someone who had a predetermined attitude about something? A predetermined attitude may sound like, "I am not smart at that" or "I don't know how to do that, so I'm not even going to try."

Each moment of life may not feel as if it is solely about your passion or bringing you joy and a passionate life. When you make a mistake, or things don't turn out how you would like, use your imagination to find what you can learn from it.

When you know what you can do, make a choice and make it happen.

Conscious choice is the key to understanding how to live fully and mindfully. Sometimes, you must respect that it is time to grow, learn and re-create. That does not mean that you cannot practice finding joy in knowing that you are experiencing in the moment the infinite possibilities of living through your own re-creation.

Try this experiment: Grab a pen and paper and place it beside you. Find a soft, comfy place where you can relax for a few minutes. Then go inside and find one of those little voices within you that needs a little encouragement. Breathe! Breathe several deep breaths while relaxing deeper and deeper. Ask the question, "How could I do that?"

or if you feel real resistance, "How could I do that, assuming I wanted to?" Guide your mind to find its own resources. Stretch your mind and imagination. Don't dismiss anything that wanders through. All things are possible here. Encourage positive self-talk such as "I can! I will stretch and grow." Keep breathing fully and completely, that's right, in and out... as you come back from your creative journey, write down all that came to mind.

• What positive self-talk can you use today?

Grab your copy of positive self-talk samples and get started today at
www.MindfulnessInActionBook.com

Your thoughts right now?

"If you want happiness, create it now. Find the joy and beauty of this moment.
Give yourself permission to be happy now.
Give yourself permission to be beautiful now.
Decide at this moment to be a leader, and you have become one. It can be that fast.
Taking responsibility is not difficult.
It is the deciding to take responsibility that is hard."

~Thomas D. Willhite~

Practice Joy

Stay attuned to the simplest events. I often carry a note pad with me and write down those moments when something really strikes a chord. Simple events can have profound effects. My most profound was a "little thing." At the time it did not seem to be much, it was two simple words that would come to impact my life more than most other events. As I sat cross-legged on a hard floor at my first Dharma Dialogue wondering why I had allowed my friend to "drag" me there, I heard, "Practice Joy."

I had never thought of joy as something one practiced. But it's true.

We practice piano, we practice a sport, so why do we not practice a fundamental component of our humanity — the art of joy?

That is the amazing thing about living mindfully in action: joy and happiness come from doing, planning, being involved and satisfied in the moment.

Be open to change.

- What would happen if you mindfully chose to practice joy?

"To laugh often and much; to win the respect of intelligent people and the affection of children; to earn the appreciation of honest critics and endure the betrayal of false friends; to appreciate beauty; to find the best in others; to leave the world a bit better, whether by a healthy child, a garden patch or a redeemed social condition; to know even one life has breathed easier because you have lived. This is to have succeeded."

~ Ralph Waldo Emerson~

The All-Too-Often Unappreciated Actions

Living mindfully does not complain about what it doesn't have, it focuses on what it has and where it's going. Focusing on something makes it bigger. This holds true for both the positive and the negative. Focus on what you want, rather than what you don't want. Be sincerely grateful for what you have already. All is there waiting to be found.

The dictionary says that gratitude is a noun, but it should be a verb. Gratitude requires action. Express gratitude at every opportunity; you never know if you will have that moment again. Consider how far just a smile and kind word will go. Take a moment right now; write down three things you are grateful for.

Look at what you have right now. What are you grateful for? Share with others what you appreciate about them? It's amazing, when you express gratitude for these, more things to be grateful for and appreciate will come to you. Cool, huh?

"Being true to yourself really means being true to all the complexities of the human spirit."

~Rita Dove~

The Gut Knows What It Knows

The gut knows what it knows. You'd be wise to trust it. Science has shown that we have three "brains": the reptilian, the mammalian and the computer brain. We also have a body brain – the gut. The neurons lining the gut are so extensive and attuned to your safety that they have been nicknamed our "second brain." Although this body brain has no known conscious thoughts or decision-making capabilities, you'd be wise to trust those gut feelings.

When you trust your body brain — your gut too, or listen to your intuition, you take responsibility for yourself, your own state of being, and your life.

I've seen it too often not to firmly believe that we know when we are being true to ourselves. So many times, we override that "gut-feeling" and talk ourselves out of "it" and right into trouble. (Now, I don't mean the type of trouble where you would be looking for bail money.) It usually is the trouble that causes uncertainty and anxiety.

Being centered in yourself is key to knowing your purpose(s). Being centered means being completely truthful with yourself by being aware of who you are and knowing what you will become.

When something doesn't feel right, sound right, seem right... it probably isn't right—at least for you. It may be right for someone else, but not you. Have the courage to say, "No, thanks." When you do say, "No, thanks," congratulate yourself for being fully present—physically, emotionally and energetically.

- What can you do right now to trust your "gut-feelings" more?

How do you know when you are centered?

"I rejoice in each moment as a new adventure. I choose to live a life of service, love and compassion, and leave this world a better place for my Being. I am here now, in this moment."

~Sharon Sayler~

Quick Survival Guide for Mindfulness in Action

No one passion or purpose has made my life whole. Living mindfully is about the courage for self-exploration, self-disclosure, re-creation and perspective. It is the conscious choice to stay in the present moment that breaks us free from our patterns and our instant reactions, allowing us to passionately, mindfully enjoy each moment.

Remember, you create what you focus on, those nasty little mind-inventions, so each time you choose, make sure it's what you want.

- Choose your intentions and goals wisely. Be choosy.

- Do the work. Be passionate.

- Try new things. Be fearless.

- Make your expectations preferences. Be humble.

- Share ideas and opinions freely. Be courageous.

- Encourage feedback and new ways of thinking. Be open.

- Take a break from judging and labeling. Be accepting.

- Most important: Check your ego at the door.

Postscript

Committing to living mindfully is serious work. It is the acceptance of conscious choices about your life.

A passionate, aware, mindful life is a chain of successful moments that become minutes, that turn into hours, evolving into days, and pretty soon, that's your life. If you choose each day to make today the most successful, happiest day of your life, you will have a passionate life.

As you have read and seen, *living mindfully* requires no starting over from scratch! Just subtle changes to the "how" you do what you already do — maybe a tweak here and there for the better – where you could be more effective, more present, more joyful, more aware and mindful!

Mindful living comes by detecting and eliminating limiting beliefs, disabling thoughts, those voices in your head that offer judgments, or the habit of labeling everything for efficiency. Remember, there is no one reality. Let go of your own hallucinations, conflicts and confusion.

You may backtrack on occasion, but having a clear understanding of the simple steps to mindful living will take you closer to your goals, passions and purposes. At times, life may feel unmanageable or you may notice something is missing. Feelings and emotions can feel overwhelming. Since you now know that it will happen, it will not be a surprise, and it's just a choice to come back to now.

Long withheld feelings or emotions can come back swiftly or integrate gradually. Honor how those thoughts and feelings choose to re-create into yourself. Acknowledge all thoughts and feelings, give grace and thank yourself.

As your awareness blossoms, it's common to get excited and want everyone to come along with you on this new adventure. However, know that people will change, they just resist being changed, so let those thoughts and feelings flow from you with a simple blessing that they will be intrigued by the re-creations all around you.

Observe your thoughts and feelings as if they were ordinary objects — how do you respond to each one now? What happens when you approach from that place of curiosity of "Isn't that interesting...?"

Whether something is possible or impossible depends on YOU. There will be both internal and external obstacles that stand in your way. You can use them as excuses for not taking action—or you can choose not to. You are not your beliefs, thoughts and feelings.

The release and healing begins as you take action and choose to physically rise up into living mindfully. Once you take mindful action, the obstacles lose their power. The actions necessary may feel difficult, embarrassing, demeaning, etc.

Realize that those undesirable qualities are, for the most part, mere inventions of the mind.

You are not what others label you. Your choice to take action in alignment with your positive intentions will work to override those mind-inventions. Be willing to courageously seek outside support from others, including family, friends and professionals, if necessary.

Dear Friend and Fellow Adventurer,

I hope you've enjoyed the "ride." Having coached hundreds of people to reach their goals, I have seen some common areas where even successful people get stuck. It's not uncommon to have more hope lost the longer you stay stuck. That is why I chose to write *Mindfulness in Action*.

To stay in the now is a choice we make over and over each day and everyone (including myself!) could always use some practice.

Practice is taking action—but what action? It's only through taking action and observing the response, yours and the world's reactions, that you will ever know the true meaning of your circumstances. It's in the meaning that you give the current situation and how you choose to react to that meaning that determines your outcome.

I shared with you that I tried to mediate for years – I couldn't sit still long enough even to stare at a TV. My beloved Aunt Myrtle used to say about my younger self, "That girl has ants in her pants!" As an adult, I've mastered neuro-linguistic programming, thought pattern management, meditation, and hypnosis along with many other techniques to see if I could command my mind to focus and stay in the moment. Through all that training, I discovered I'm a kinesthetic learner and for me the best way to be mindful is to be in action: my best ideas come either in the shower or while cleaning house. But those are only ideas until I get feedback as I chose to act on those ideas and in turn, observe others in the moment as they experience their now, from a different viewpoint. And it's the Four-minute Meditation that allows me to calm my mind and reset my energies.

Practice the four-minute Meditation, a couple of times a day, or more if you like. It's worked wonders for me and fits in my busy, "ants in the pants" schedule. You can download an mp3 and Action Sheet for your own Four-minute Meditation at www.MindfulnessInActionBook.com if you haven't tried it yet I really encourage you to.

Even though we humans are built to be part of a tribe, don't let other people or ideologies tell you who you are — they are just to provide you a greater understanding of the whole experience.

Vetting those "best" ideas with others is how I understand the impact I have or don't have. It's only when the loop is closed in how you choose to act and react and how the worlds reacts that you learn whether your awareness is true or not.

What meanings do you place on your experiences?

I remember the first time I visited Paris I couldn't wait to see the Louvre Museum. I was chattering non-stop in sharing with my traveling companion all the wonders I wanted to see there and none more than the Mona Lisa painting. I knew it would be even more amazing than all the other items I'd viewed that day.

The moment came as I turned the corner to the room that housed the famous painting... I was dumbfounded. The room is huge and the painting so small, a mere 21 inches by 31 inches. I had expected to be awestruck.

Once I recovered from my surprise and the huge crowd, I quickly became awestruck as I viewed it from the front of the line. You see, in that moment I remembered that the reason I wanted to see the painting (my "why") had not changed.

Why do I share this experience? I could have left the museum that day sad and forlorn. Remember, mindful action is not the experience; it is the meaning you attach to the experience.

So let's entertain all ideas whether you choose a new action, a change, or not. You may find some or all of the ideas I share here in *Mindfulness in Action* are easy to implement in one area of your life and not so easy in another. That is common.

Continue to play and observe the meaning you place on it. Try any or all ideas... feel free to discard what doesn't work for you or store it away. You never know what may work at a later time or what you may be able to share with others. When I don't understand something I take a mental note and store it in my "Isn't that Interesting?" file to come back to at a later time.

I only ask you to commit to putting your heart, head and soul into the moment and make the choice to entertain the ideas presented here — play with them — see how they work in your life. But remember, if you only set your mind to change, change rarely happens.

We change only within the way we view the world; if we continue to view the world the same way, nothing will change. That's why I suggest you "play" with change.

The reason change often feels hard is not the experience of change; here again, it is the meaning or the story you attach to change. The reason why you are changing is the meaning and if the meaning is not your choice, change often comes about as something we have to do. And who likes to do something they HAVE to do?

Yet, when we "play" with something, as in take a physical action, we experience it from a different point of view. Different points of view, whether we get them from others or us approaching something with play, give us a different meaning about the change.

Remember to download your free copy of the thought provoking questions on the action and strategy sheets at

www.MindfulnessInActionBook.com

As you play through the ideas, tips and techniques that have worked for myself and others, enjoy, play and practice the art of being present in the moment... practice joy, practice observing, play with your awareness of the little things going on around you, practice mindful action.

You never know when small things will have profound effects. Surprise yourself!

Only by taking mindful actions based on what you've discovered on the inside and outside will you find where you gain the knowledge, clarity and focus to achieve your desired destiny and a life worth living.

The choice is yours to make: mindful action or not. Yet, I encourage you to choose to explore your courage, imagination, creativity, wonder and curiosity as you create, recreate, transform and renew your passions for and in life and align with your purposes.

Seek out mentors to help you develop your special purposes, gifts and passions that make you— YOU.

For me, I truly stand on the shoulders of greatness. I have been blessed by many rich mentorships and friendships. I am eternally grateful to all my "teachers" too numerous to mention (whether they know it or not) for their influence on me. It's through that combined inspiration, motivation and encouragement that I am able to use my given talents.

221

I acknowledge and thank all of you who have touched my life, taught me and allowed me to share with you on your journey of discovery of your goals and dreams. You have paved my way with joy. I am forever in your debt. I hope this book paves the way for others, including you, to find joy.

I'd enjoying meeting you over at our supportive community: The *Mindfulness in Action* Society at http://www.MindfulnessInActionBook.com

We are all about continued personal development, no matter what place you are at in your life. There is always something to learn or share. The aim of *Mindfulness in Action* is to not change anything about you—you are a perfect being, complete and whole, just the way you are, if that's what you choose. Its purpose is to continue to explore this grand adventure of life together!

Life's short. Take Mindful Action now.

Live each moment, whatever your adventure!

Warm regards,

Sharon

P.S. Let's cut to the chase and talk about results. Change can be unsettling, but it all is in how you structure change; join me today over at www.MindfulnessInActionBook.com/ to learn more.

Praise For Mindfulness In Action

"Once again, Sharon Sayler did not disappoint! I have been following Sharon Sayler's work for years, and know her as an outstanding coach who has the ability to break down complex issues into bite size, easy to digest pieces. The outstanding principles she teaches in *Mindfulness In Action* are applicable to anyone who would like to create a peaceful life amidst the chaos in our world today. An excellent read."

~ Viki Winterton,
Founder, Expert Insights Publishing

"Sharon Sayler's book cuts through the noise and distraction of modern life and gives you the tools to have mindfulness everyday. I felt more peace and awareness in my life just reading chapters in her wonderful book than I have in years."
~ Mike Michalowicz, Author of *Profit First*

"In today's world we rush about trying to do so much and yet never really stopping to appreciate the moments. Whether that be to watch the wind blowing in the trees, a child showing us their latest creation or what a friend or partner is telling us.

We can all fall so easily into the technology trap with our heads down looking at the latest piece of information on our smart phones and we forget what is around us. Those 'real life' moments can be lost forever unless we really take time out and engage again.

Sharon's wonderful book will take you through the process of coming 'back to life' and why we all need to cherish those moments away from our busy lives, not only for health benefits but also for the benefit of the world around us.

Sharon teaches us how to look up again and engage once more with what is happening around us. Sharon you are a star and thank you for bringing me 'back to life' again."

~Simon Jordan
Founder of One Planet One Place

"There is a duality to life. Life must have both stillness and constant change. However, when we live life mindfully, our actions reflect it, which then brings us the life experiences we truly seek. Sharon Sayler takes us deeper into this truth and natural way of being, through her words and wisdom. Press pause… your life will be enriched by this book."
~ Laura Simonson

Acknowledgments

Appreciation and gratitude bring joy to me. Joy in being connected to life. Joy in the realization that there is a larger context in which my personal story continues to unfold. I have attempted to write many times. Without the love and encouragement of these out- standing individuals listed, this book would not have come about.

First and foremost, much love and appreciation to my sons, Adam and Jordan, to my parents, Don and LaMae; my sisters, Linda and Janene; their husbands, Lowell and Michael; and to David who nourishes my soul and is a never-ending reflection of love and understanding; and finally much appreciation to the unsung hero of the group, my editor and friend, Deedee Pegler.

I have been blessed by many rich friendships and I am eternally grateful to all my "teachers" too numerous to mention (whether they know it or not) for their influence on me. It's through that combined inspiration and encouragement that I am able to use my God-given talents. I acknowledge and thank all of you who have touched me, taught me and entrusted me with your goals and dreams.

I truly stand on the shoulders of greatness. You have paved my way with joy. I am forever in your debt. I hope this book paves the way for others to find joy.

Warmest regards,

Sharon Sayler
Author of *Mindfulness in Action*
http://www.MindfulnessInActionBook.com/

About the Author

As a communications consultant and CEO of Competitive Edge Communications, Sharon Sayler, MBA, ACC works with professionals to enhance their leadership, relationships, self awareness, and verbal and non-verbal skills to achieve their personal and professional goals. A sought-after speaker, Sharon teaches others to make conscious and courageous choices to create the life they want and deserve.

Learn more about Sharon and her work at

http://www.MindfulnessInActionBook.com and http://www.SharonSayler.com.

Be sure and tune into Sharon's latest radio show and podcast archive to hear the latest from http://www.LifeInterruptedRadio.com. A show dedicated to putting hope in your heart and health and well-being in your body, mind and soul.

ISBN 0-9818177-1-8

Mindfulness in Action: A Hands-On Guide to Creating Peace Amidst the Chaos

© 2014 by Sharon Sayler

www.MindfulnessInActionBook.com

JURNEE PUBLISHING

PO Box 68689, Portland, OR 97268
Connect@MindfulnessInActionBook.com

855.909.6100